The

 PRET

RECIPE BOOK

★

EMMA HARDY

The PRET RECIPE BOOK

★

HOW TO MAKE

fantastic

SALADS
and
SANDWICHES

★

PAN BOOKS

First published 1996 by Pan
an imprint of Macmillan Publishers Ltd
25 Eccleston Place,
London SW1W 9NF
and Basingstoke

Associated companies throughout the world

ISBN 0 333 34830 2

1 3 5 7 9 8 6 4 2

A CIP catalogue record for this book is available from
the British Library

Typeset by Parker Typesetting Service, Leicester
Printed and bound by Mackays of Chatham plc, Chatham, Kent

This book is dedicated to
Pret's remarkable employees,
the very lifeblood
of our company.

Many thanks Nellie and Emma,
without whom this book
would never have got
off the ground

CONTENTS

Foreword

Part One
SALADS

Part Two
SANDWICHES

The very first branch of Pret A Manger opened in 1986 – we are now on schedule to open our fiftieth store by Christmas 1996. Over the last ten very hectic years we have learned a tremendous amount. Whilst much of Pret's retail strategy has evolved and developed, a number of our core values have never needed altering. The first of these is always to use good-quality, fresh ingredients, which makes the difference between a good sandwich and a great one. Easier said than done, I can assure you.

We have, over the years, dreamt up and introduced hundreds of sandwich and salad ideas into our range. Some have stood the test of time, others haven't. This book contains a mix of the old and the new as well as the Pret Classics – all of them quick and easy to make and every one delicious. We hope you enjoy them.

If you would like to speak to me or one of my colleagues regarding anything to do with Pret A Manger, please feel free to call on 0171 827 6300.

Thank you

Julian Metcalfe

Part One

 PRET™

THE SALADS

★

THE SALADS

1 New Potatoes in a Creamy Dressing 13

2 Watercress, Tomatoes, Black Olives 14

3 Red, Green and Yellow Peppers 16

4 3-Bean Mix with Leeks, Lemon, Capers and Coriander 18

5 Oriental Noodles, Sesame, Ginger, Spring Onions, Coriander 20

6 Guacamole 22

7 The Classic Waldorf 24

8 Fresh Peas, Broad Beans, Pancetta, Spring Onions,
Tarragon and Mint 26

9 Pret's Famous Tuna Pasta 28

10 Pasta with Red Pesto Dressing 30

11 Wild Rice, Pinenuts, Lemon Zest, Chervil, Fresh Herb Dressing 31

12 Mixed Leaves with a Fresh Herb Dressing 32

13 Orzo or Arborio, Prosciutto, Fresh Peas 34

14 Tabbouleh: Tomato, Cucumber, Onion, Mint, Lemon, Parsley 35

15 Wild Rice, Red Onion, Sugar Snap Peas 36

16 Pasta with Smoked Salmon 37

17 Steak, Rocket and Balsamic Vinegar 38

18 Turkey, Red Onion, Lime, Avocado 39

19 Chicken and Tarragon Salad with a Strong Mustard Dressing 40

20 Spicy Shrimp with Fresh Chilli, Glass Noodles, Sorrel and Leeks 42

21 Spicy Chicken, Radicchio, Cucumber, Yoghurt, Mint 44

22 New Potatoes, Bacon, Pinenuts 46

23 Green Beans, Pancetta, Chervil, Walnut Oil 47

24 Tuna, Borlotti Beans, Spring Onions 48

THE SALADS

25 **The Perfect Lentil Salad** 49

26 **Oriental Prawn, Ginger, Soy, Sesame, Spring Onion, Sugar Snap Peas** 50

27 **Bacon and Egg Salad** 52

28 **Salade Niçoise** 54

29 **Caesar Salad** 56

30 **Pret's Version of the Chef's Salad** 58

31 **Bacon and Avocado with Mustard Dressing** 59

32 **Mozzarella, Plum Tomato, Avocado, Basil** 60

33 **Grilled Goats' Cheese with Mesclun** 62

34 **Greek Salad** 63

35 **Cottage Cheese, Broccoli, Black Olives** 64

36 **Ricotta and Feta, Tomatoes, Pumpkin Seeds** 65

37 **Parmesan, Rocket, Fennel with a Lemon Dressing** 66

38 **Stilton, Pear, Walnuts, Radicchio with a Creamy Dressing** 67

39 **Fennel, Tarragon, Broad Beans with a Walnut Dressing** 68

There is an amazing selection of salad leaves these days. Often the supermarkets provide the biggest choice, and most salad leaves are available all year round. You can buy whole lettuces or ready prepared leaves packed in plastic bags. Most supermarkets offer a good selection of both. Lettuces definitely taste better in the summer, which is their natural season for growth, and you'll find that their price drops a bit as well. Here's our guide to the leaves that are widely available.

We've divided the leaves into two sections: *sturdy* and *delicate*. The delicate leaves have to be handled gently as they bruise easily. They must be spun dry, or drained thoroughly in a colander or sieve, then spread out on a towel. And they certainly need to be dressed just before you eat them or you'll end up with a salad that looks soggy and wilted.

Sturdy Leaves

Cos   Sweet, crisp, long leaves with an excellent flavour. Keeps well too. Take care to remove the thick central spine from the larger leaves – these can be hollow and are too bulky for sandwiches and unattractive in salads. The inner leaves, paler in colour, are even sweeter. Cos is essential for Caesar salad, and makes any other salad better than average. When buying Cos lettuce, look out for ones which are a healthy green with firm leaves, dense and heavy.

Little Gem   A small but close relation of Cos. All leaves are crisp and good, and Little Gem is widely available all year round. Usually available in packs of two or three, check that they are nicely green and unwilted before buying them.

Radicchio   Round, tightly packed red lettuce with a slightly bitter (but very good) flavour. Its flavour can be improved by shredding the leaves. (Cut the radicchio in half, top to bottom, cut out the tough white core at the base, then slice the radicchio finely, cutting across its width.) When buying radicchio, look out for firm, heavy, tightly packed heads and avoid those whose outer leaves are going limp and brown.

THE ENDIVE FAMILY

Chicory (Belgian Endive)   These pointed fleshy leaves are grown in the dark, which accounts for their pale yellowy white appearance. Sometimes the tips of the leaves are green which means they have found some light somewhere, but this doesn't seem to affect their taste much. They should be firm, juicy and crunchy. The flavour is pleasantly bitter and they can be sliced finely, or simply split in half and the leaves detached from the stalk.

Curly Endive (Frisee)   Mad-looking, frizzy frilly lettuce whose pale inner leaves are deliciously crunchy and full of flavour. Discard the dark outside leaves; these can be bitter and tough. Make sure that the lettuce you buy is crisp and unwilted, and has a large proportion of pale inner leaves. Endive lettuces are particularly good with a mustardy dressing.

Escarole   Large spreading lettuce – a smooth version of curly endive. The darker green outside leaves are bitter, so make sure the lettuce is heavy with plenty of pale yellowy green inner leaves which are wonderfully crisp. Discard the outer leaves and wash the rest thoroughly. Lasts well in the fridge for up to three days, as do the other endive lettuces.

Delicate Leaves

Oak Leaf   Quite expensive, but a wonderful leaf for mixed salads because of its attractive bronze leaves. Wash and dry carefully.

Lambs Lettuce   Small fragile clumps of green leaves with a mild taste. Wash them well; the roots and stalks hang on to a lot of grit (they are usually grown in sand). Best used in mixed salads because of its price, although a salad composed entirely of lambs lettuce is a delicate luxury.

Rocket (aka Arugula or Roquette)   Dark serrated leaves usually sold ready trimmed from their stalks. Rocket is now available in most super-markets and greengrocers, and even if you don't see it on the shelves, try to order it as most retailers are happy to oblige. It has a marvellous strong peppery flavour and can be used to spike a green salad or as a luxurious accompaniment to cheese, fish, red meat, etc. When you buy rocket, whether it has been pre-packed or not, make sure the leaves aren't floppy, bruised or wilted and make sure that it *is* rocket and not young spinach leaves, as some retailers have mistakenly offered.

Young Spinach   Leaves up to 3 in/8 cm long are suitable for eating raw in salads. Make sure the leaves are fresh looking and unbruised and wash them thoroughly – spinach tends to be muddier than most other leaves.

Watercress   At best this has a wonderful peppery taste and, like rocket, it's a great asset to green salads. Use only the leafy ends, and if the watercress seems very stalky with tiny leaves don't buy it unless you're desperate. Whether you buy it in bags or bunches, make sure that the leaves are a deep green and smooth, not soggy or wilted. Store watercress bought in bunches upside down (leaves submerged) in water in the fridge. Bags of watercress last a few days in the fridge (careful not to let them touch the side of the fridge or the watercress might freeze, which ruins it). Wash watercress in cold water, pinch off any thick stalks and pick out any leaves that are discoloured or soggy-looking.

The following lettuces are, in our opinion, not really worth buying: Lollo rosso and Lollo bianco (both these have zero taste); Chinese leaf (crisp but insipid); Iceberg (totally tasteless, but it is crunchy and keeps well in the fridge because of its high water content, so buy it if you're desperate).

Tossing and Dressing Salads

It is best to dress leaf salads just before you're about to eat them. Most salad leaves don't last well once they're covered in oil – they taste good but start to look rather limp and bashed about.

The best way to toss leaf salads is with your hands. This way you can be sure that the more delicate leaves don't get bruised and that everything gets well coated in dressing. Be gentle. The larger your salad bowl, the easier it is to toss the salad well without it overflowing on to the table.

Herbs

Fresh herbs are easily available all year round and these are our Top Eight.
1. *Tarragon* – brilliant aniseed/liquorice flavour, can overpower other herbs, so best used on its own or with parsley or chives.
2. *Basil* – usually the deeper green the leaves, the stronger they taste.
3. *Mint* – look out for the deep green smooth leaves and avoid pale hairy ones.
4. *Chives* – don't buy limp ones.
5. *Parsley (flat leaf/Italian/continental)* – it really does taste better than the frizzy kind.

6. *Dill* – feathery fern-like herb which is particularly good with cucumber and fish.
7. *Coriander* – some people find this rather overpowering, but its strong, slightly pungent taste is wonderful in oriental and South American-inspired salads.
8. *Chervil* – a fine and feathery cross between tarragon and parsley.

For the salad recipes in this book there are only a few oils, vinegars and seasonings that we would like you to consider. This is our Top Ten:

Extra virgin olive oil　Italian olive oils, particularly those from Tuscany and Umbria, have a strong taste (so use them sparingly) and often – depending where they come from – a wonderful green colour. Look out also for Greek extra virgin oil; this can be just as good (Mani oil, available from branches of Sainsbury's and Tesco is delicious).

　　Don't store olive oil in the fridge, it will become cloudy and viscous. If this happens, let it warm to room temperature and it will return to its normal state. Keep it tightly sealed and away from direct heat and light, and once opened use within a few months.

Plain olive oil　This is a blend of milder tasting olive oils which is more suitable for cooking when olive oil is required.

Walnut oil　This has an amazing taste, and brings a mild salad to life. It tastes wonderful with cheeses such as goat, and is essential if you want to make the best Waldorf salad. Once opened it must be stored in the fridge otherwise it will quickly become rancid.

Sunflower oil　This can be combined with extra virgin olive oil for most salad dressings in order to lighten the dressing. (Dressings made only with extra virgin olive oil are heavy and can even become bitter.) Also useful for light cooking and stir frying. Store in the same way as olive oil.

Red or white wine vinegar and sherry vinegar　These are as good as each other and pretty much interchangeable, so choose whichever one you prefer.

Balsamic vinegar　This seems to be an essential part of anyone's kitchen these days; it is a magical, dark and syrupy vinegar made from the concentrated juice of white grapes and matured in a series of wooden casks. Very small amounts make a huge difference to a salad. It will keep for a long time if you store it in a cool, dark place, tightly sealed, and it is well worth buying. Look out for bottles which are marked Aceto balsamico di Modena. As long as you buy from a reputable store, these should be the real thing.

Hellman's Mayonnaise   This is still, we think, the best easily available mayo you can buy. And they make a pretty good reduced-calorie version too. This said, most of the leading supermarkets offer good own-brand mayonnaises.

Dijon mustard   If you have to choose one mustard, make it Dijon. It's great in salad dressings, with cold meats and, mixed with Hellman's, makes an excellent mayonnaise. Lots of people swear by Colman's English mustard and this shouldn't be ignored, but it can overpower other salad ingredients so that you forget they're there.

Maldon sea salt   This is wonderful and available from good supermarkets. The salt crystals are fairly large and flaky, but they can be crumbled between thumb and forefinger when a small amount is wanted. It really does taste better than ordinary table salt. Buy this and you'll see why we insisted.

Black pepper   Black pepper must be freshly ground and the peppercorns themselves must be as fresh as possible. It makes all the difference in the world. If they've been sitting around for ages, throw them out and buy some new ones. If you haven't got a pepper grinder, try to get one; or, if the worst comes to the worst, smash whole peppercorns wrapped in a tea towel using a hammer. When buying black peppercorns look out for Tellicherry peppercorns, available from good foodshops and delicatessens.

There are hundreds of different dressings you can make, and hundreds of variations on a theme. The most simple and basic dressing is the vinaigrette. This is a mixture of oil and vinegar and a little seasoning. French dressing is a vinaigrette with a little mustard. Obviously there are so many oils and vinegars available and so many opinions on how to make a vinaigrette that results can vary enormously. (Rumour has it that if ever you visit a deserted part of the world, be sure to take some oil and vinegar with you. If you feel lonely, start to make a salad dressing and people will appear from nowhere, all of them telling you that you're doing it wrong!)

Follow this guide for a fail-safe and delicious vinaigrette:

1 tbsp extra virgin olive oil	1 pinch Maldon sea salt
1 tbsp sunflower oil	1 pinch freshly ground black
1 tsp red or white wine vinegar	pepper

Combine all the above in a clean bowl or jam jar and whisk with a fork (or screw the lid firmly on the jar and shake). Or you can make the dressing directly in the salad bowl before adding the salad ingredients.

For a French dressing, add ½ teaspoon of Dijon mustard to the vinaigrette recipe.

Stock

This crops up in a number of our recipes. In most cases a small amount is needed (1–2 tbsp). Unless you have an ever-ready bowl of home-made stock try to buy Marigold bouillon powder. You can make up exactly the quantity of stock you need in an instant. A pinch of powder makes one or two tablespoons of stock.

Beef

At the time of going to press the BSE beef scare was at its height. Any beef that Pret A Manger uses is thoroughly checked (our Pastrami, for instance, is made from South American grass-fed beef). We avoid gelatin at all costs. We recommend you buy beef from a highly reputable source, ensure that it is grass-fed, free-range, organic if possible, and steer well clear of cheap cuts and 'reclaimed products'.

1

NEW POTATOES IN A
CREAMY DRESSING

Serves 4

Look out for the small pink potatoes called Roseval. At the end of the summer Pink Fir Apple potatoes hit the supermarket shelves; these are wonderful too. Otherwise buy the newest, smallest potatoes you can find (from May onwards); Jersey Royals are good. Charlotte potatoes seem to be available for most of the year and these are excellent in this salad. If they seem large, cut them in half.

I lb (475 g) new potatoes	freshly ground black pepper
sea salt	2 tbsp crème fraîche
I tbsp olive oil or I oz (30 g) butter	2 tbsp mayonnaise
I tsp finely grated lemon zest	small bunch chives

1   Clean the potatoes in cold water using a scrubbing brush. Cut away any bruised or dark patches. Put them in a saucepan, cover with cold water, add a large pinch of sea salt.

2   Bring to the boil, turn the heat to medium and cook, three quarters covered to allow the steam to escape, for 20–30 minutes, depending on the size of the potatoes.

3   Drain the potatoes, put them back into the hot saucepan with either the butter or olive oil (or both!), the lemon zest, another good pinch of sea salt and a lot of freshly ground black pepper. Stir them about so they become coated with oil/melted butter.

4   In your serving bowl, put the crème fraîche and mayonnaise (you can use low-fat versions of these, if you prefer) and whisk together with a fork.

5   Add the potatoes and the chives, chopped into ½ in/1 cm lengths, and stir everything about so that the potatoes are thickly coated. It's important you do this while the potatoes are still hot.

6   Serve hot, warm or at room temperature.

★   *If you can resist eating the potatoes all at once, store them in the fridge (they will keep for a couple of days) and let them warm up to room temperature again before eating them.*

WATERCRESS, TOMATOES, BLACK OLIVES

Serves 2

This is a wonderful side salad: it goes brilliantly with pasta, fish, meat, risotto, quiche, cheese on toast – almost anything – and can take the place of any vegetables. Eat it on the same plate as your main dish, or on its own with warm bread and butter.

2 large tomatoes
2½ oz/75 g black olives, preferably marinated
(½ tsp Herbes de Provence – these are only necessary if the olives have not been marinated in herbs)
2 bunches fresh watercress or 1 2½ oz/75 g bag

for the dressing:
1 tsp finely grated lemon zest
2 tsp balsamic vinegar
2 tbsp extra virgin olive oil
pinch of sea salt
freshly ground black pepper

1   Peel the tomatoes by scoring a small cross on the bottom of each tomato with a sharp knife and then covering them with boiling water for 30 seconds. Cool them under a running cold tap; the skins should peel off easily. Cut them in half, remove the pips and the tough white pith at the top, then slice them roughly and put in the salad bowl.

2   Remove the stones from the marinated olives by tearing the olives in half (they will be soft from the marinade and easy to handle), the stones will almost fall out. Add the olive halves to the tomatoes in the bowl. If the olives are not marinated and have had their stones removed, cut or tear them in half and add them to the tomatoes along with half a teaspoon of Herbes de Provence (Schwartz brand are good quality and widely available).

3   Add the grated lemon zest, the balsamic vinegar, the olive oil, a pinch of Maldon sea salt and quite a few grinds of black pepper. Mix thoroughly and leave to stand at room temperature (ideally for an hour) until you are ready to eat.

4   Prepare the watercress at the last minute and spin or drain dry. Pinch off any thick stalks and remove any discoloured or limp leaves. Add the watercress to the bowl and toss well, using your hands. Eat immediately.

LEMONS Quite a few of the recipes in this book call for fresh lemon zest and juice. We recommend that you try to buy unwaxed or, best of all, organic lemons when zest is required. The zest of waxed lemons will include large quantities of varnish used to enhance and preserve their appearance as well as untold pesticides. Always give lemons a good wash before you use them and wipe them dry with a tea towel. To obtain the zest use the fine side of the grater or a zester if you have one. Be careful not to grate deeper than the skin – the white pith can be bitter.

Try to buy thin-skinned lemons – they have a smoother shape and tend to be smaller than their knobbly counterparts. Thin-skinned lemons are juicier and sweeter and their zest has more zing as well as less pith. Choose lemons which feel firm and heavy and avoid pale green ones which aren't fully ripe. Store lemons at room temperature.

OLIVES We think black (fully ripened) olives are best. They are sweeter and juicier than the unripe green olives which are often sharp and bitter as well as being indigestible. Black olives are also more suitable for marination. It doesn't matter whether or not they have had their stones removed as long as they haven't been preserved in salt. Try to buy olives preserved in oil rather than brine or, worst of all, vinegar (you will never get rid of the vinegary taste).

Home marinated olives are sensational. If you feel like giving them a go, here's how:

MARINATED BLACK OLIVES

1 tbsp balsamic vinegar
1 tsp black peppercorns crushed in a mortar and pestle, or with the back of a wooden spoon
6 cloves fresh garlic, peeled and scored

4 bay leaves, torn in half
1 green or red chilli pepper, fresh or dried, roughly chopped
2 thick slices of unwaxed or organic lemon, roughly chopped
½ lb/225 g black olives
2 tsp Herbes de Provence
olive oil

Mix together the vinegar, peppercorns, garlic, bay, chilli and lemon. Stir in the black olives and the Herbes de Provence. Put them into a large jam jar and add enough olive oil to cover the olives. Put the lid on tightly and keep at room temperature, out of direct heat and light for a few weeks.

RED, GREEN AND YELLOW PEPPERS

Supermarkets sell packs of 3 assorted peppers which are ideal for this recipe. If you are buying them loose, choose small peppers, no larger than 10 cm/4 in.

1 red sweet pepper
1 green sweet pepper
1 yellow sweet pepper
2 tbsp olive oil
1 plump clove fresh garlic, finely
    chopped
sea salt
freshly ground black pepper
1 tbsp freshly squeezed lemon juice
½ tbsp caster sugar
1 red onion

for the dressing:
1 heaped tbsp small capers
1 tbsp extra virgin olive oil
½ tbsp balsamic vinegar
pinch Maldon sea salt
freshly ground black pepper
small handful coriander leaves or
    flat parsley leaves, roughly
    chopped

1 Cut the peppers in half lengthways. Remove the stalks, cores, seeds and white membranes. Cut the peppers lengthways into thin strips (max. ½ cm).

2 Put 2 tablespoons olive oil into a frying pan. Add the pepper strips, the chopped garlic, a sprinkle of salt and some freshly ground black pepper. Cook over a fairly high heat for about 5 minutes, adding the lemon juice about halfway through.

3 Top and tail the onion and remove the outside papery skin. Cut in half and slice each half into fine segments.

4 When the peppers are starting to soften in the pan (5 minutes), add the onion and sugar, stir, and cook for another 4–5 minutes. The onion and peppers should start to caramelize a little.

5 Turn off the heat, and add all the ingredients for the dressing to the peppers and onions in the pan. Move everything around so that all the ingredients combine, then pour into a salad bowl.

★ *This pepper salad is excellent with pasta – just add it as it is to the hot drained pasta. Or toast/grill 2 thick slices of bread, rub the toast with a peeled garlic clove and pile the warm pepper salad on top.*

SWEET PEPPERS   Yellow peppers are the sweetest and juiciest, followed by red. Green peppers are unripened red peppers. Choose firm peppers with a smooth regular shape and even colour. Avoid overripe peppers with soft spots. Weigh the pepper in your hand and choose those which feel heavy for their size: an indication of thick and juicy flesh. Wash under a running tap and wipe dry with a tea towel before preparing them.

GARLIC   Choose firm unsprouted bulbs of garlic with large cloves that are tightly wrapped in white or pinkish purple parchment-like skin. The heavier a bulb or head of garlic feels in the hand, the fresher it is likely to be. Avoid bulbs that are dried out, bruised, yellowed or soft. Store garlic in a cool, dry place (never in the fridge) and leave it in its skin until you are ready to use it.

To peel a clove of garlic, crush it lightly with the back of a wooden spoon, then trim off the base with a sharp knife and the rest of the skin should come away easily. Rub a peeled and crushed clove around the salad bowl before making the salad and it will have a hint of garlic. Slice and chop garlic finely, or grate it for a strong taste. Alternatively use a garlic press (more convenient for recipes such as guacamole) which squeezes out the oil and gives a very strong, almost pungent taste. The best way to prepare garlic is to pound it in a mortar and pestle with a pinch of sea salt.

SMALL GREEN CAPERS   These are the buds of a climbing Mediterranean plant. They are sold in small jars and are widely available from supermarkets. Unfortunately they are usually preserved in vinegar which alters and sharpens their flavour. Drain and rinse them thoroughly and, if possible, soak them in a little olive oil before use. Once a jar of capers is opened, store it in the fridge and the capers will last for ages.

The larger Italian capers, which are stocked only in good delicatessens and ethnic grocers, are often preserved in salt. Although they taste better they must be soaked in water for 15 minutes and then rinsed thoroughly under a running tap or they will be too salty.

★ 4   3-BEAN MIX WITH LEEKS,   Serves 2
LEMON, CAPERS AND CORIANDER

This is quite a filling salad and is best eaten warm, perhaps with some crusty bread and a few green leaves tossed in walnut oil. Tinned beans are suitable for this recipe.

4 oz/110 g butter beans
4 oz/110 g black-eye beans
4 oz/110 g red kidney beans or
   borlotti beans
1 leek
1 tsp butter/olive oil
2 tbsp capers
2 tbsp fresh coriander leaves,
   washed, dried and chopped
   roughly (flat-leaf parsley or
   tarragon)

for the dressing:
$\frac{1}{2}$ lemon
3 tbsp extra virgin olive oil
sea salt
freshly ground black pepper
1 tbsp stock (optional)

1   If you haven't bought ready-cooked beans (available almost everywhere in tins) *see opposite* for how to prepare and cook dried ones.

2   Trim and wash the leek (*see opposite*) and slice into very fine rings. You will need 3 or 4 heaped tablespoons of sliced leek. Melt a teaspoon of butter or olive oil in a frying pan and stir-fry the leek slices for 2 minutes or so. They won't be thoroughly cooked but they will have lost their rawness.

3   Add 2 tablespoons of drained capers (*see notes on page 17*) to the leek slices in the pan.

4   Grate some lemon zest and squeeze the juice of $\frac{1}{2}$ lemon over the leeks in the pan, add 3 tablespoons olive oil, a pinch of sea salt and some freshly ground pepper. Add most of the chopped coriander (save some for sprinkling on the finished salad), stir everything around – this is the salad dressing.

5   Put the drained cooked beans into your salad bowl (if they are still warm, so much the better) and pour everything from the pan over the beans. Toss the beans gently so that they don't become mushy but are thoroughly coated with the leek and caper dressing. If the salad seems too dry, add a tablespoon of stock. Scatter the remaining coriander over the top and serve.

★   *A clove of fresh pink garlic, peeled and squeezed through a press or finely chopped, added to the pan of leeks will make the bean salad taste more robust.*

Some freshly cooked bacon, broken into pieces and stirred into the warm salad will make it even more substantial.

DRIED BEANS   Many supermarkets and certainly all health food shops sell wide selections of dried beans. Most of them need soaking for 24 hours, in several changes of water, before you cook them. The ready-cooked beans in tins are good and labour saving, so it may be worth paying a bit extra, but remember to rinse them thoroughly before using them to get rid of their tinning liquid.

Dried beans double their size and weight once cooked, so if you want to cook exactly the amount for this salad, weigh out 2 oz/55 g of each of the three bean varieties. They have to be soaked separately because they need cooking for different lengths of time. Soak them overnight in cold water. Change the water first thing in the morning and leave them soaking in fresh water until you are ready to use them later that day. (A quicker method, suggested by Lynda Brown, is to boil the dried beans furiously for 10 minutes in plenty of water and let them stand in this water to soak for 3 to 4 hours. They are then ready for cooking.)

The beans are ready to cook when they've doubled in size and their skin is plump and smooth. If the skins are still wrinkled, they'll need more soaking.

Put the fully soaked kidney beans into a saucepan and cover with water. Bring to a fast boil and boil furiously for 15 minutes. Turn the heat down and let them simmer for another 15 minutes. Drain them and return them to the empty pan along with the fully soaked butter beans and black-eye beans. Cover the lot with fresh water, bring to the boil and cook on a medium heat, three quarters covered for half an hour. All the beans should be ready now.

Borlotti beans don't need the 15-minute fast boil, but they need cooking for 1 hour, so add the butter beans and black-eye beans halfway through the cooking process.

Drain the beans and place in salad bowl. Now they're ready for the dressing.

TRIMMING AND WASHING LEEKS   Leeks hang on to an awful lot of grit, so they must be thoroughly washed. Trim off ½ in/1 cm from the root end and remove the outer layer or two of skin from the leek. Split the leek open, from top to bottom, and hold it under a cold running tap with the dark green end pointing downwards. Rinse meticulously, lifting up the layers and sluicing the grit and mud away. Shake off the water and close the leek up again before you chop it.

ORIENTAL NOODLES, SESAME, Serves 2
GINGER, SPRING ONIONS,
CORIANDER

Sharwood's egg noodles (thread or medium), or rice (glass) noodles are easy to find and perfect for this salad. Or you could try Clearspring's 40 per cent or 100 per cent SOBA, authentic Japanese Buckwheat noodles.

5 oz/150 g dried noodles	*for the dressing:*
1 tbsp sesame oil	4 tbsp sesame oil
3 spring onions	2 tbsp soy sauce
fresh root ginger	1 tbsp freshly squeezed lemon juice
2 tsp sesame seeds	1 tbsp freshly squeezed lime juice
½ cucumber	1 fresh clove garlic, peeled and finely chopped
2 tbsp coriander leaves, thoroughly washed and dried, chopped roughly	1 shallot, peeled and finely chopped
	1 heaped tsp freshly peeled and grated ginger
	1 tsp horseradish *or* ¼ tsp wasabi
	pinch sea salt
	freshly ground black pepper

1   Cook the noodles according to the instructions on the pack, usually a 3-minute boil. Drain and put them in your salad bowl with a tablespoon of sesame oil to stop them from sticking together.

2   Trim, wash and slice (diagonally) the spring onions, using the dark green part as well as the white. Throw on top of the noodles.

3   Peel a bit of root ginger the size of a hazelnut and grate it over the noodles.

4   Toast the sesame seeds – either dry-fry them in a frying pan until golden brown, or put them under the grill for a minute or two. Add some of them to the noodles and save the rest to scatter over the top of the salad before serving.

5   Peel the cucumber with a potato peeler. Slice not wider than ¼ in/½ cm and then cut the slices into thick matchsticks and add them to the noodles.

6   Add some of the coriander to the noodles, save the rest for scattering on top before serving.

7   Whisk all the dressing ingredients together in a bowl, or put them in a mini-blender and whizz for a minute.

8   Toss the noodles, spring onions, etc, together. Pour the dressing over the noodles, toss gently, scatter the remaining sesame seeds and coriander on top and serve.

★   *You can add any number of steamed or stir-fried vegetables to the noodles – or serve them alongside. Consider sugar snap peas, leeks, broccoli, courgette, shredded cabbage, pak choi and bean sprouts.*

GUACAMOLE

We find the greyish green mush usually passed off as guacamole unappetizing. Here's our version which looks and tastes impeccably fresh.

2 ripe (but not too soft) avocados, preferably Hass
1 lime
½ tbsp sunflower oil
½ tbsp extra virgin olive oil
2 plum tomatoes or medium-sized vine-ripened tomatoes
½ medium-sized red onion

1 fresh red or green chilli pepper (widely available from supermarkets and greengrocers)
1 firm clove garlic
pinch sea salt
freshly ground black pepper
1 tbsp freshly chopped coriander

1 Peel the avocados, remove the stones (see *opposite*) and chop the flesh into small roughly shaped cubes.

2 Squeeze the juice from the lime into a bowl. Add the oils, whisk briefly with a fork, and then add the avocado. Scoop all the juice over the avocado using a spoon, to prevent it from discolouring.

3 Peel the tomatoes: score a small cross on the bottom of each tomato with a sharp knife, immerse them in boiling water for 30 seconds. Drain. Cool under a running tap. Slide the skins off, remove any white pith and most of the seeds, chop roughly into cubes the same size as the avocado and add to the bowl.

4 Remove the outside skin from the onion, chop roughly into small pieces and add to the bowl.

5 Prepare the chilli pepper (see *opposite*). Depending on the size of the chilli and your own taste use half or all of the flesh. Chop very finely. Add to the bowl.

6 Peel the garlic clove and squeeze through a garlic press if you have one. If not, crush it with the back of a wooden spoon and then chop finely, adding a small pinch of salt. Add to the bowl.

7 Sprinkle a pinch of sea salt and five or six grinds of black pepper. Add the chopped coriander.

8 Using a spoon, carefully combine all the ingredients so that they are well mixed and covered with lime juice, but avoid the dreaded 'mush' look.

9 Leave to stand for up to half an hour before eating so that all the flavours combine.

10 Serve with hot bread, tortilla chips, pitta bread, or coarse-cut toast rubbed with fresh garlic.

AVOCADOS   There are several varieties, of which the Hass is probably the best. It has hard, knobbly black skin and its flesh is smooth, buttery and tastier than most. Check for ripeness by squeezing the top end gently – it should give slightly without being soft. Smooth-skinned avocados such as the Fuerte can be tested in the same way but do not buy any that have mottled skins or dark bruises – these are damaged and overripe and will taste sour.

The flesh of a perfectly ripe avocado should be pale and creamy greenish yellow. Buy them a few days in advance and ripen them at room temperature. You can hold ripe avocados in the fridge for a day or two, to slow down further (over)ripening, but let them warm to room temperature before eating them.

To peel and de-stone an avocado, use a sharp knife and cut in half from top to bottom, sliding the knife around the stone. If you manage to embed the knife in the stone, you can twist the two halves of the avocado away, leaving the stone attached to the knife. (It can take ages trying to prise a slippery stone from half an avocado.)

FRESH CORIANDER   This is widely available in supermarkets and easily confused with flat-leafed parsley until you get close enough to smell it. It has a very distinctive, almost pungent smell. It is mainly used in Thai and Mexican cooking (hence its inclusion here).

CHILLI PEPPERS   There are many many varieties of chilli peppers. The most commonly available fresh chillies are green or red (green = unripe, red = ripe) known as Dutch Red chillies. These are the shape and size of small fat carrots. Another type, known as Thai Hot, is very thin and curved and has a much hotter taste. The Dutch Red are the best ones to use here: buy ones that have smooth unwrinkled skin. They can be stored in the fridge, preferably in a paper bag to stop them from flavouring other food, and will stay fresh for up to a week.

To prepare, wash under a cold tap and wipe dry. Cut the top off the chilli, slice down the middle, remove the white pith and seeds from the inside, then chop the flesh finely.

NB: Please be careful not to touch your face or rub your eyes while handling chillies as they will burn and irritate sensitive areas. Best to wash your hands thoroughly in cool soapy water after you've finished chopping.

★ 7 **THE CLASSIC WALDORF** Serves 2

This simple salad of chopped apples, celery and walnuts was created at the Waldorf Hotel in New York. You can add Little Gem lettuce, slivers of poached chicken breast and Belgian endive if you want to make it more substantial. But we think it's best at its simplest . . .

3 oz/85 g walnut halves (18–20
   whole nuts)
1 tsp butter
sea salt
freshly ground black pepper
2 Granny Smith apples
½ head celery (approx. 6 good
   crisp sticks)

for the dressing:
1 heaped tbsp live natural yoghurt
1 heaped tbsp mayonnaise
freshly squeezed juice of ½ lemon
1–2 tbsp walnut oil
pinch of sea salt
freshly ground black pepper
1 tbsp balsamic vinegar

1   Whether you are cracking the nuts yourself or have bought them ready shelled, check the walnut halves for any of the tough membranes that may have been left on and remove them. Chop the walnut halves roughly and put them in a small saucepan with a teaspoon of butter, a pinch of sea salt and a few grinds of black pepper. Stir them around over a medium heat until the butter has fully melted, the nuts are beginning to sizzle a bit and there is a wonderful toasty smell. If you're short of time, use the walnut pieces as they are; however the extra time spent pan-frying the walnuts is well worth it. Remove the pan from the heat and set aside while you:

2   Wash and wipe dry the apples. Cut them into quarters and cut out the pips and core from each quarter. Cut the quarters in half again lengthways and cut each of these segments into three or four pieces. Place them in your serving bowl.

3   Scrub the celery under a running tap and wipe it dry. If the stalks are wider than 1 in/2½ cm cut them in half lengthways. Then cut all the stalks into small slices at an angle, max. ½ in/1 cm wide.

4   Mix all the dressing ingredients together using a fork and pour the dressing over the apples and celery. Add the walnut pieces and toss everything together. Dribble the balsamic vinegar over the salad just before you eat it. It will bring it to life.

5 Eat immediately, or leave it in the fridge for half a day or so – the flavours will have combined even better – but remember to let it warm up to room temperature before eating it. Cold food straight from the fridge doesn't taste anything like it does when it's at room temperature.

★ *A tablespoon of roughly chopped fresh tarragon leaves added to the dressing isn't authentic but does taste brilliant. This salad is a good Christmas-time snack, delicious served alongside cold turkey, or with turkey added to it; also there are always plenty of walnuts around at Christmas!*

★ 8   FRESH PEAS, BROAD BEANS, Serves 2–4
PANCETTA, SPRING ONIONS,
TARRAGON AND MINT

This is a summer salad. When you see fresh peas and broad beans in their pods stacked on the greengrocers' shelves make this salad and hope it's warm enough to eat outside.

1 lb/475 g peas in their pods
1 lb/475 g broad beans in their
   pods
or 6 oz/170 g each of frozen peas
   and broad beans
2 thick slices pancetta or medium-
   smoked bacon
1 tsp butter or olive oil
1 red onion
2 spring onions
$\frac{1}{2}$ pint/290 ml stock (see page 11)
1 heaped tbsp fresh tarragon
   leaves, thoroughly washed and
   dried
1 heaped tbsp fresh mint leaves

for the dressing:
2 tbsp extra virgin olive oil
1 tbsp fresh lemon juice
$\frac{1}{2}$ tbsp balsamic vinegar
1 tsp caster sugar
pinch sea salt
freshly ground black pepper

1   Shell the peas and broad beans. If the broad beans are larger than a fingernail, remove the pale green outer skin as well. It's a bit time-consuming but really worth it.

2   Cut the rind off the pancetta and cut into matchstick slices using a pair of scissors. Put them in a saucepan over a medium heat with a teaspoon of butter or olive oil and start to fry.

3   Peel the red onion, and slice lengthways into slim segment slices. Peel the outside skin from the spring onions, rinse the onions under the tap, and slice lengthways into 2 or 3 long strips. Add these to the pancetta, which should be nearly cooked by now and stir-fry for another few minutes.

4   Turn the heat up full, add the peas and broad beans and the stock, bring to the boil, then turn the heat down to medium, cover the pan and cook the peas and beans for 2 minutes.

5   Remove the pan from the heat and let it cool for half an hour. If there is too much liquid, spoon some of it off. Add the tarragon and mint leaves and stir around so that they wilt slightly in the warmth of the pan and give out their flavour.

6   Put the contents of the saucepan into a salad bowl, make the dressing in a separate bowl and pour it over the top.

★   *You can serve this warm, on toast rubbed with a little fresh garlic as a starter, or use it as a delicious sauce for freshly cooked pasta.*

★ 9   PRET'S FAMOUS TUNA PASTA   Serves 2

Our best-selling pasta salad, delicious hot or cold, served with some green leaves tossed in a mustard vinaigrette. If you want to make the tuna pasta a little lighter, substitute fromage frais for the mayonnaise, and use only 1 tablespoon olive oil and 2 tablespoons chicken or vegetable stock.

3½ oz/100 g tin dolphin-friendly
    tuna, preserved in brine
½ fresh unwaxed or organic lemon
2 heaped tbsp mayonnaise
1 leek
1 small red onion
1 tsp butter or olive oil
2 tbsp capers
1 tsp fresh thyme leaves

2 tbsp extra virgin olive oil
4 oz/110 g fusilli pasta
2 tbsp black olives
½ cucumber
2 heaped tbsp flat-leaf parsley
    leaves, thoroughly washed and
    dried
freshly ground black pepper

1   Drain the tuna, and put it in your salad bowl with 1 teaspoon of freshly grated zest from the half lemon and most of the juice. Break up the tuna chunks with a fork, add the mayonnaise and stir everything together.

2   Trim and wash the leek (see page 19), peel and finely slice the red onion and put them in a frying pan with a teaspoon of butter or olive oil. Stir-fry for a few minutes until they start to go soft. Add the capers and the thyme leaves. Stir for another minute or so, remove from the heat and leave to cool in the pan.

3   Squeeze the remaining lemon juice over the leek and onion, and add the 2 tablespoons olive oil, scraping all the juices from the pan and stirring together.

4   Cook the pasta for 13 minutes or so in plenty of boiling water. Drain and add to the tuna mix in the bowl. Pour everything from the frying pan over the pasta and tuna and mix it all together.

5   Remove the stones from the olives, (see page 15 for notes on olives) and add to the tuna pasta.

6   Peel the cucumber and cut into small chunks. Add to the pasta.

7   Chop the flat-leaf parsley roughly and add half the amount to the pasta.

8   Give everything a good toss so that the pasta is really well coated with tuna. Scatter the remaining parsley on top, grind on some fresh black pepper, and serve hot or cold.

DRIED PASTA OR FRESH PASTA?   Both are good, the choice is yours. When buying dried pasta (which is factory made from 100 per cent durum wheat flour and water) look for these makers: Voiello, Di Cecco, Barilla. Pasta should be cooked in plenty of ready boiling water. The more water that surrounds it the better and more evenly it cooks and the less likely it is to stick together in the pan. Most makers specify cooking times on their packets, but in general the finer shapes (spaghetti, linguine, trenette) should boil for 8 minutes, while the thicker shapes (penne rigate, rigatoni, fusilli) need about 13 minutes. You want your cooked pasta to be al dente rather than soft.

Fresh pasta is made from the same flour as dried pasta but with eggs instead of water. It is yellower in colour and slightly sweeter and richer in taste. It cooks in half the time of dried pasta. Most of the large supermarkets now offer really good fresh pastas. They can be frozen at home until you are ready to cook them. Many Italian delicatessens sell fresh pasta made on the premises. This hardly needs cooking at all (especially if it's fresh that day) and is best eaten at its simplest with butter or olive oil, a little seasoning and fresh herbs or lemon zest.

You can also buy an expensive dried pasta made with eggs which, if cooked correctly, is identical to fresh pasta.

PASTA WITH RED PESTO DRESSING

Serves 2

You can buy red pesto in jars from most supermarkets. If you can find it, then use it instead of the ingredients listed under red pesto dressing.

1 small leek
1 small red onion
½ courgette
1 tsp butter
1 tbsp stock
4 oz/110 g fusilli pasta
1 small red pepper, grilled, skin removed (see page 85)
2 heaped tbsp flat-leaf parsley
Parmesan cheese
2 tbsp toasted pinenuts
pinch sea salt
freshly ground black pepper

for the red pesto dressing:
1 heaped tbsp mayonnaise
1 heaped tbsp fromage frais or crème fraîche
1 heaped tbsp freshly grated Parmesan
1 tbsp condensed tomato puree
2 oz/55 g sun-dried tomatoes, roughly chopped
2 tbsp stock
2 tbsp extra virgin olive oil

1   Trim, wash and slice the leek. Peel and slice the red onion. Wash, wipe dry, and slice the half courgette into matchsticks. Put all of them into a frying pan with one teaspoon butter or olive oil and stir-fry for a few minutes until they start to soften. Add a tablespoon of stock.

2   Cook the pasta for about 13 minutes in plenty of boiling water. Drain and put in your salad bowl with a little olive oil to prevent it from sticking together. Add the leek, onion and courgette from the pan. Add the roughly chopped grilled red pepper.

3   Wash, dry and chop the flat-leaf parsley. Add most of it to the pasta.

4   Combine all the ingredients for the red pesto dressing in a bowl and whisk together, or put them into a mini-blender and whizz for half a minute. Pour the dressing over the pasta and toss, *or* add 3 or 4 heaped tablespoons of red pesto from a jar to the pasta and toss.

5   Shave some Parmesan over the pasta using a potato peeler or the wide slice on a grater.

6   Toast the pinenuts either under the grill or dry fry them in a non-stick pan until they are golden brown. This will take 2–3 minutes. Scatter the toasted pinenuts over the red pesto pasta along with the remaining parsley, add seasoning, and serve.

WILD RICE, PINENUTS, LEMON ZEST, CHERVIL, FRESH HERB DRESSING

Serves 2–4

The toasted pinenuts emphasize the wonderful nutty flavour of the wild rice. You can eat this warm or cool and perhaps serve it on a bed of green leaves. Wild rice is expensive, so you can substitute half the quantity of wild rice for some long-grain brown rice; they can be cooked together.

4 oz/110 g wild rice (Tilda wild rice is widely available)
½ fresh unwaxed or organic lemon
handful (1 oz/30 g) fresh chervil
2 tbsp toasted pinenuts
1 tbsp walnut oil

for the dressing:
2 heaped tbsp fresh flat parsley leaves

1 tbsp fresh tarragon leaves
2 tbsp chopped chives
1 tsp fresh sweet marjoram leaves
2 tbsp walnut oil
1 tbsp natural live yoghurt
juice from the ½ lemon
sea salt
freshly ground black pepper

1 Wash the wild rice in several changes of cold water. Put in a saucepan with double the volume of fresh water, cover with a lid, bring to the boil and simmer for 45 minutes. Check the pan after about half an hour; you may need to add more water. The wild rice should have doubled in size and most of it may have split. Take the pan off the heat and leave it, covered, to cool down.

2 Grate the zest from the half lemon (see page 15).

3 Wash and dry the chervil thoroughly. Be gentle – it's very delicate. Remove any thick stalks.

4 Toast the pinenuts either under the grill or dry fry them in a non-stick pan until they are golden brown. This will take 2–3 minutes.

5 *The dressing:* either put all the ingredients into a mini-blender and whizz for a minute *or* chop all the fresh herb leaves in a mug or jam jar using scissors and then whisk in the other ingredients.

6 Drain the rice and put it in a serving bowl with the lemon zest, toasted pinenuts and chervil and an extra spoonful of walnut oil. Toss gently.

7 Spoon the herb dressing over the top.

★ *Delicious with cold meat or fish, or simply on its own in a lunchbox.*

MIXED LEAVES WITH A FRESH HERB DRESSING Serves 4

This is delicious and simple and relies on totally fresh good-quality ingredients. This recipe will serve at least 4 people on the basis that it's worthwhile preparing a large quantity of the salad leaves at a time. You can serve it in two halves, store the leaves in a damp tea towel in the fridge and the dressing in a jar with a lid. Both will keep fine for a couple of days.

1 Cos lettuce or 2 Little Gem
   lettuces
1 curly endive or Escarole lettuce
1 oak leaf lettuce
1 oz/30 g baby spinach or lambs
   lettuce
1 oz/30 g rocket
handful of fresh chervil
sea salt

for the dressing:
10 large fresh basil leaves
1 tsp fresh sweet marjoram leaves
1 tsp fresh thyme leaves
2 tbsp fresh flat parsley leaves
1 tbsp freshly squeezed lemon juice
freshly ground black pepper
2 tbsp extra virgin olive oil
1 tbsp walnut oil
1 tbsp sunflower oil
1 tbsp natural live yoghurt

1 The sturdy leaves: remove and discard the outer leaves from the Cos/ Little Gems and the curly endive/Escarole. Then remove all the inner leaves from the central stalk down to and including the heart and wash thoroughly in cold water. Cut away any tough or large stalks and tear the larger leaves into pieces the size of the smaller leaves (approx 2–2½ in/5–6 cm long). Spin dry or drain and pat dry in a tea towel.

2 The delicate leaves: remove and discard the outer leaves from the oak leaf lettuce. Remove the inner leaves from the stalk and wash them thoroughly in cold water along with the baby spinach/lambs lettuce, rocket and chervil. Pinch off any thick stalks and pick out any discoloured or limp leaves. If some leaves are very large you may need to tear them in half but bear in mind that all these leaves bruise easily: the less done to them the better. Spin dry or drain first in a colander or sieve and then spread out on a tea towel.

3 Put all the above in a large salad bowl and toss, using your hands so the leaves are mixed together. Sprinkle a pinch of sea salt over the leaves.

4   *The dressing*: put all the fresh herb leaves into a cup or jam jar and snip at them using scissors until they are finely chopped. This is a quick, easy and effective way to chop fresh herbs. Add the lemon juice and a few grinds of black pepper, then whisk in the 3 oils and finally the yoghurt.

5   Pour the dressing over the leaves, toss thoroughly and eat immediately.

ORZO OR ARBORIO, PROSCIUTTO, FRESH PEAS

This is almost like a cold risotto and travels extremely well (picnics, lunchboxes). Orzo is dried pasta shaped like rice grains, Arborio is one of the polished white rices used for making risotto. Choose whichever you prefer – the main difference is that Arborio rice, once cooked, will absorb the dressing very quickly, so if you are travelling, don't dress the salad until the last minute.

1 red onion

1 tsp butter/olive oil

Herbes de Provence

4 oz/110 g of freshly shelled peas (buy 8 oz/225 g of peas in their pods) *or* 4 oz/110 of thawed frozen peas

½ pint/290 ml stock – chicken or vegetable

2 oz/55 g prosciutto or Parma ham or jambon de Bayonne

4 oz/110 g Orzo pasta or Arborio rice

1 stock cube for cooking rice

for the dressing:

3 tbsp extra virgin olive oil

1 tbsp red or white wine vinegar

1 heaped tbsp fresh mint leaves

1 heaped tbsp fresh flat parsley leaves

1 heaped tbsp fresh chopped chives

1 heaped tbsp fresh tarragon leaves

sea salt

freshly ground black pepper

1   Make the dressing either in a mini-blender (whizz everything together for 1 minute) or in a jar or mug. Put all the herb leaves in the jar, snip them with scissors until they're finely chopped, then add the other ingredients and whisk everything together using a fork.

2   Top and tail the red onion and peel off the outside layer of papery skin. Cut into fine segment-shaped slices. Put it in a saucepan with a teaspoon of butter or olive oil and a pinch of Herbes de Provence and fry gently until the onion starts to become translucent, turning golden at the edges. Turn the heat up high, add the peas and the stock and cook fast for 2 or 3 minutes.

3   Cut the prosciutto into thin strips using scissors.

4   Cook the Orzo pasta in plenty of boiling water for about 8 minutes or whatever it says on the packet. Drain. *Or* cook the Arborio rice for 20 minutes in double its volume of water into which you've dissolved a vegetable or chicken stock cube. Drain.

5   In either case, add the peas, onion and stock from the pan and stir into the rice. Add the prosciutto strips and the herb dressing, toss well and serve.

★ 14   TABBOULEH: TOMATO,   Serves 2–4
CUCUMBER, ONION, MINT, LEMON, PARSLEY

Tabbouleh is made with cracked wheat, also known as bulgar wheat, and is extremely simple to prepare. If you can't find cracked wheat, use couscous which is made from durum wheat semolina and is equally easy to use.

4 oz/110 g bulgar wheat or
    couscous
1 tsp butter
pinch of sea salt
freshly ground black pepper
2 perfectly ripe tomatoes
½ cucumber
½ fresh organic or unwaxed lemon
1 small red onion
2 heaped tbsp fresh mint leaves

2 heaped tbsp fresh flat parsley
    leaves

for the dressing:
2 tbsp extra virgin olive oil
2 tbsp sunflower oil
1 tbsp freshly squeezed lemon juice
pinch sea salt
freshly ground black pepper

1   Bring 4 fl oz/110 ml water in a pan to boiling point. Add the bulgar wheat or couscous with a heaped teaspoon of butter, a pinch of sea salt and some freshly ground black pepper. Stir it well with a fork. Cover the pan and remove from the heat. Leave it to stand for 10 minutes. It will swell and absorb all the water. Give it another stir with the fork to break up the grains.

2   Peel the tomatoes (unless they are organic in which case wash them and wipe them dry) by making a small cross with a sharp knife at the bottom of each tomato and immersing them in boiling water for 30 seconds. Their skins will peel away easily. Chop into smallish pieces, about the size of sugar lumps.

3   Peel the cucumber and chop into sugar lump-sized pieces.

4   Cut a quarter lemon into sugar lump-sized pieces, removing any pips.

5   Top, tail and peel the outside skin from the red onion. Chop finely.

6   Chop the fresh herbs roughly.

7   Put the bulgar wheat or couscous into your salad bowl and add everything else you have chopped.

8   Whisk together the dressing ingredients and pour over the tabbouleh. Toss everything together gently.

★   *Prepare at least an hour before you eat to allow the flavours to combine.*

WILD RICE, RED ONION, SUGAR SNAP PEAS

Serves 2–3

Very simple and, once the rice is cooked, very quick. You can add a perfectly ripe avocado if you want to make this a bit more substantial. This salad travels extremely well.

4 oz/110 g wild rice
1 red onion
1 tsp butter/olive oil
pinch Herbes de Provence
6 oz/170 g fresh sugar snap peas

for the dressing:
1 heaped tbsp fresh sweet marjoram leaves
1 heaped tbsp fresh mint leaves
1 tbsp extra virgin olive oil
2 tbsp walnut oil
1 tbsp freshly squeezed lemon juice or red/white wine vinegar
pinch sea salt
freshly ground black pepper

1   Wash the wild rice in several changes of cold water. Put it in a saucepan with double the volume of fresh water, cover with a lid, bring to the boil and then turn down to simmer for 45 minutes. Check the pan after about half an hour; you may need to add a little more water. The wild rice should have doubled in size and most of it may have split. Take the pan off the heat and leave it, covered, to cool down.

2   Top and tail the onion and remove the outside papery skin. Slice it into very fine segment slices and stir-fry these briefly in a pan with a teaspoon of butter or olive oil and a pinch of Herbes de Provence.

3   Wash and drain the sugar snap peas, and top and tail them, peeling away any string from the spine of the pods. If you have a vegetable steamer, steam the sugar snap peas for 2½ minutes only, or cook them in a little boiling water for 2 minutes. In either case, don't add the sugar snap peas until the water is boiling. Start timing the moment the sugar snap peas hit the boiling water/ steam. Remove them from the steamer or pan immediately and put them in your salad bowl.

4   Chop the fresh herbs very roughly using a pair of scissors and whisk together with the other dressing ingredients.

5   Drain the wild rice and add to the sugar snap peas along with the red onion and the dressing. Toss thoroughly and leave to stand for half an hour or so before serving.

★ 16 **PASTA WITH SMOKED SALMON** Serves 2–3

This looks beautiful and is equally delicious hot or cold.

2 fresh plum tomatoes
4 oz/110 g smoked salmon
small bunch fresh chives
2–3 tbsp crème fraîche
4 oz/110 g penne rigate pasta (see page 29)

2 tbsp extra virgin olive oil
freshly ground black pepper
sea salt
fresh lemon juice

1 Peel the tomatoes: cut a small cross at the bottom of each tomato, immerse them in boiling water for 30 seconds, then cool under a running tap – the skin will peel off easily. Cut them in half lengthways. Remove all the pips and tough white pith at the stalk end if there is any. Cut them into $\frac{1}{4}$ in/$\frac{1}{2}$ cm strips lengthways (use scissors – it's quicker). Set aside.

2 Cut the smoked salmon into $\frac{1}{4}$ in/$\frac{1}{2}$ cm strips (again scissors are easier). Set aside.

3 Cut the chives using scissors into $\frac{1}{2}$ in/1 cm lengths. You will need about 3 tablespoons. Add most of these to the crème fraîche and mix together.

4 Cook the pasta in plenty of boiling water for 9 minutes or so (follow pack instructions) if it's dried, less if it's fresh. Drain and place in a large salad bowl with a tablespoon extra virgin olive oil, some freshly ground black pepper and a small pinch of sea salt (remember smoked salmon is usually quite salty so don't overdo it). Stir it around – the oil will prevent the pasta from sticking.

5 Add the crème fraîche and chives, stir together.

6 Add the tomato and smoked salmon strips.

7 Toss everything together with a spoon and fork, add another tablespoon of olive oil, a quick squeeze of lemon juice and an extra grind or two of black pepper. Scatter the remaining chopped chives on top.

★ *If you are serving this hot, grate or shave some fresh Parmesan over the top.*

STEAK, ROCKET AND BALSAMIC VINEGAR

Serves 2

This is a wonderful and very quick supper for meat lovers. It needs no accompaniment but if you're really hungry cook some new potatoes and serve with butter and pepper, or bake some potatoes and serve with sour cream and fresh chives.

2 large handfuls (2 oz/55 g) fresh
  rocket
sea salt
2 tbsp balsamic vinegar
2 tbsp extra virgin olive oil

1 large lean rump steak, organic if
  possible 6–8 oz/170–225 g
1 tbsp Dijon mustard
1 tbsp fresh thyme leaves
freshly ground black pepper
1 tbsp butter

1   Wash and spin dry the rocket, taking care to pinch off any thick stalks and remove any discoloured or limp leaves. Put it in your salad bowl, sprinkle it with sea salt, 2 tablespoons balsamic vinegar and 2 tablespoons of extra virgin olive oil and toss gently.

2   Cut off any thick fat from the steak, spread with $\frac{1}{2}$ tablespoon Dijon mustard, $\frac{1}{2}$ tablespoon of thyme leaves and 1 or 2 grinds of black pepper.

3   Heat 1 tablespoon butter in a frying pan. When the butter is really hot (but not burnt) put the steak, mustard side down, into the pan and cook over a high heat for 3 minutes. During that time, spread the upperside with the rest of the mustard, thyme and a little more black pepper. Turn the steak over and cook for another 3 minutes. Turn the heat off and let the steak cool in the pan. It will continue to cook and its juices will release into the pan, making a wonderful gravy which you will pour over the salad.

4   After about 5 minutes remove the steak from the pan and cut it into slim strips, about $\frac{1}{2}$ in/1 cm wide. You can do this with scissors, holding the steak over the bowl of rocket so that any juice drips on to the salad.

5   Arrange the strips over the rocket, pour the juices from the pan over the top, serve and eat immediately. Unbelievably delicious.

TURKEY, RED ONION, LIME, Serves 2
AVOCADO

The idea for this salad comes from a wonderful Mexican soup called Sopa di Lima – lime soup. It is traditionally made with turkey which is eaten all year round in Mexico and served with fresh tortillas. This salad, therefore, has a natural accompaniment – tortillas or polenta. You can also toss some crisp green leaves such as Cos in a mustard vinaigrette to serve alongside, or just add the leaves to the turkey salad and eat the lot together.

1 red onion	freshly ground black pepper
8 oz/225 g freshly cooked turkey breast	1 heaped tbsp fresh coriander leaves
4 oz/110 g sugar snap peas	1 heaped tbsp fresh flat parsley leaves
1 fresh lime	
1 perfectly ripe avocado	2 tbsp extra virgin olive oil
sea salt	1 heaped tbsp natural yoghurt or fromage frais
pinch paprika	

1   Top and tail the onion and remove the papery outer skin. Cut in half and slice each half into fine segments. Rinse thoroughly under a cold tap to remove some of the onion's sharpness. Drain well and place in salad bowl.

2   Cut the turkey meat into narrow strips and add to onion in salad bowl.

3   Wash, top and tail the sugar snap peas. Steam or boil them in a little water for $1\frac{1}{2}$–$2\frac{1}{2}$ minutes, no more (in either case, don't add the sugar snap peas until the water is boiling. Start timing the moment the sugar snap peas hit the boiling water/steam). Drain them and add them to the turkey and onion in the bowl. Squeeze the juice from half the lime over everything.

4   Peel, de-stone and slice the avocado. Add to the salad bowl.

5   Sprinkle a pinch of sea salt, a pinch of paprika and 2 or 3 grinds of black pepper over everything. Chop the herbs with scissors and scatter over salad.

6   Whisk together the olive oil, yoghurt and the juice of the other half of the lime and pour over the salad. Toss gently and serve.

★   *If you want to be really authentic and spice this up a little, chop half a de-seeded Dutch Red chilli pepper very finely and scatter over the salad before you dress and toss it.*

★ 19   CHICKEN AND TARRAGON   Serves 2–4
SALAD WITH A STRONG
MUSTARD DRESSING

Served warm or cold, summer or winter, this is a classic you'll want to make again and again.

1 medium-sized red onion
1 large Cos lettuce
2 freshly cooked chicken breasts
    (see *opposite*)
2–3 heaped tbsp fresh tarragon
    leaves

for the dressing:
1 tbsp Dijon mustard
$\frac{1}{2}$ tbsp red or white wine vinegar
2 tbsp extra virgin olive oil
1 tbsp sunflower oil
1–2 tbsp mayonnaise
pinch sea salt
freshly ground black pepper
1 tbsp freshly squeezed lemon juice

1   Peel the papery outer skin from the red onion and cut in half, top to bottom. Place each half face down and cut into thin segments, slicing lengthways. Put into a bowl, cover with cold water and refrigerate for at least half an hour. This removes some of the sharpness from the onion.

2   Remove the tougher outer leaves of the lettuce and discard. Remove the inner leaves from the stalk. Wash thoroughly in cold water, tear the larger leaves into smaller pieces, spin dry, or drain and roll in a tea towel.

3   Cut or tear the chicken breasts into bite-sized pieces.

4   Make the salad dressing in the bottom of the salad bowl. Whisk together the mustard and vinegar, then add the oils, the mayonnaise, seasoning and lemon juice.

5   Chop the tarragon leaves roughly and add to the dressing.

6   Add the chicken pieces to the dressing in the bowl and toss well so that they are well coated with tarragon dressing.

7   Drain the red onion thoroughly, and add to the chicken, along with the Cos lettuce.

8   Toss lightly and serve.

CHICKEN Try to buy free-range chickens. They taste much better than their intensively farmed relations. If you can find organic chickens or Poulet de Bresse buy those, they are even better. If you are roasting a whole bird, used leftover meat for the salad opposite.

If you buy (free-range) chicken breasts, here's how to cook them for the best and juiciest results. To poach 2 chicken breasts you will need:

I tbsp butter
all or any of these herbs:
   I sprig fresh thyme
   I sprig fresh rosemary
   I bay leaf
I carrot, cleaned and roughly
   chopped
I stick celery, cleaned and roughly
   chopped

I small brown-skinned onion,
   peeled and roughly chopped
(I clove fresh garlic, peeled and
   crushed; $\frac{1}{2}$ apple, sliced – these
   are optional but they do add a
   wonderful flavour)
$\frac{1}{2}$ pint/290 ml chicken or vegetable
   stock

Melt the butter in a frying pan. Place the chicken breasts and the herbs in the pan and cook over a fairly high heat for 2–3 minutes. Turn the chicken breasts over and while the other sides are browning, add all the chopped vegetables. Cook for a further 2 minutes, then add the stock.

You can either:
Turn down the heat, cover the pan, and cook the chicken breasts in the frying pan, turning them over now and again and checking to see that there is enough stock – if necessary adding a tbsp or two of hot water.
or
Transfer everything into a small ovenproof casserole with a lid or kitchen foil over the top and cook in a moderate oven (350°F/180°C/Gas mark 4) for half an hour.

Let the chicken breasts cool in their juices and leave them there until you are ready to use them.

SPICY SHRIMP WITH FRESH CHILLI, GLASS NOODLES, SORREL AND LEEKS

Serves 2

When sorrel is available (look out for it in the fresh herb section of supermarkets during the summer) it makes this salad very fresh-tasting. If you can't find it, use rocket leaves instead. This is an ideal light supper or starter served with a few green leaves tossed in a fresh lemon dressing.

8 oz/225 g peeled prawns or shrimps
$\frac{1}{2}$ fresh unwaxed or organic lemon
1 fresh Dutch Red chilli pepper
1 clove fresh pink garlic
sea salt
1 fresh leek, long and slim
6–8 fresh sorrel leaves (or rocket leaves)
4 oz/110 g glass (rice) noodles (Sharwoods Stir-Fry noodles or Thread Egg noodles)

2 tsp butter or olive oil
$\frac{1}{2}$ tsp paprika/cayenne pepper
stock (optional)
freshly ground black pepper

for the fresh lemon dressing:
2 tbsp extra virgin olive oil
1 tbsp fresh lemon juice
1 tsp freshly grated lemon zest
pinch sea salt
freshly ground black pepper

1   Peel the prawns/shrimps if they're not already peeled, remove the dark vein that runs down the back and put into a bowl.

2   Grate the zest from the half lemon (reserving some for the lemon dressing) and squeeze most of the juice over the shrimps.

3   Wash, dry, top and tail the fresh red chilli. Split it open down its length and remove the pith and seeds. Chop the flesh very finely. You will need about 2 teaspoons of chopped chilli – more if you like things very hot.

4   Peel the clove of garlic (crush gently with a wooden spoon before cutting away the stalk end – the skin will come away easily) and chop very finely with a pinch of sea salt.

5   Trim the leek, remove the outer layer of skin and wash very thoroughly (see *page 19*). Chop into very fine slices, cutting at an angle. Use some of the darker green part as well as the white.

6   Wash and dry the sorrel leaves. Roll them into a cigar shape and slice finely. Let the cigar unfurl into shreds of sorrel.

7   Put the noodles in a bowl and cover with boiling water or stock. Leave to stand for 5 minutes.

8   Make the dressing by combining all the ingredients.

9   Heat 2 teaspoons of butter or olive oil in a frying pan. When it's melted and sizzling (don't let it become black or start smoking) add the sliced leek and the shrimps with half a teaspoon of paprika or cayenne pepper and stir-fry for 1 minute. Add the lemon zest, the chopped chilli and garlic and continue to stir-fry for 2 or 3 more minutes. If the shrimps were uncooked they should now be creamy white, tinged with pink.

10   Drain the noodles thoroughly and add to the frying pan. Toss everything together and pour into your salad bowl. Season with sea salt and freshly ground black pepper. Toss again and add 2 or 3 tablespoons fresh lemon dressing. Serve at once.

★ 21   SPICY CHICKEN, RADICCHIO,   Serves 2
CUCUMBER, YOGHURT, MINT

This is a salad version of sandwich no. 6 on page 86. You can prepare the chicken, yoghurt and mint the day before – they will taste even better – and throw everything together at the last minute. Delicious served with wild rice salads nos. 11 and 15.

$\frac{1}{2}$ cucumber

sea salt

1 lump fresh root ginger, the size of a walnut

1 fresh plump clove garlic

1 fresh Dutch Red chilli pepper

2 chicken breasts

1 tbsp sunflower oil

5 cloves

1 tsp mild curry powder

4 heaped tbsp natural (Greek) yoghurt

2 tbsp fresh lemon juice

2 heaped tbsp fresh mint leaves

1 tbsp walnut oil

freshly ground black pepper

1 small firm head radicchio

1   Peel the cucumber using a potato peeler. Cut into slices no thicker than $\frac{1}{4}$ in/$\frac{1}{2}$ cm and cut these into matchsticks. Put them in a bowl, sprinkle with some sea salt and put in the fridge for a few hours or overnight.

2   Peel and grate the fresh ginger. Peel, crush and chop the garlic. De-seed and chop the chilli.

3   Cut the chicken breasts into long strips, no wider than $\frac{1}{2}$ in/1 cm.

4   Heat 1 tablespoon sunflower oil in a frying pan. Add the ginger, garlic, chilli and cloves and fry for 1 minute. Add the chicken strips and fry over a medium heat for 3 or 4 minutes. Sprinkle the curry powder over the cooking chicken and continue to stir-fry for another 3 minutes. Add 2 to 3 tablespoons of water, stir everything together, turn off the heat and let the chicken cool in the pan.

5   Whisk 2 tablespoons of the yoghurt and 1 tablespoon of the lemon juice together. Pour this over the cooled chicken in the pan and toss thoroughly so that the chicken is completely coated. You can prepare this in advance and keep it in the fridge overnight in a bowl covered with clingfilm. Remember to let the chicken warm up to room temperature before you use it.

6   Chop the mint roughly and whisk together with the remaining 2 tablespoons yoghurt, walnut oil, 1 tablespoon lemon juice and seasoning in the bottom of your salad bowl.

7 Remove the outside leaves from the radicchio and cut out the tough white core. Shred the leaves very finely and add to the salad bowl. Toss so the leaves are thoroughly coated in dressing.

8 Drain any liquid from the bowl of cucumber slices and scatter them over the radicchio.

9 Add the spicy chicken slivers to the salad bowl, give everything one final toss and serve with warm poppadoms or nan bread.

NEW POTATOES, BACON, PINENUTS

Serves 2–3

Use thick-cut lightly smoked or sweet bacon (see *page 76 for notes on bacon*) or pancetta. Look out for Roseval (pink) potatoes, Charlotte potatoes and Fir Apple potatoes.

8 oz/225 g new potatoes	2 tbsp pinenuts
1 tsp butter/olive oil	Herbes de Provence
1 heaped tbsp crème fraîche	1 fresh Cos or Escarole lettuce
sea salt	French dressing (see *page 11*) made
freshly ground black pepper	with Dijon mustard
4 oz/110 g bacon or pancetta	

1   Cook the new potatoes in plenty of boiling water for 20 to 25 minutes. If a fork slides into their flesh easily, they're done. Drain them and put them back in the saucepan with a teaspoon of butter or olive oil, the crème fraîche, a pinch of sea salt and 2 or 3 grinds of black pepper.

2   Cut the rinds off the bacon. Using scissors, cut the bacon into ½ in/1 cm strips and put them into a frying pan. Dry-fry them over a medium heat until the fat begins to run. Turn the heat up a little, drain off any excess fat, and add the pinenuts with a pinch of Herbes de Provence. Keep moving everything around so it doesn't burn, and continue cooking until the bacon becomes nicely crisp and the pinenuts have turned a golden brown.

3   Pour the bacon and pinenuts over the potatoes and shake the saucepan so that everything gets mixed together.

4   Trim, wash and spin dry the lettuce, removing any thick stalks and discoloured or limp leaves. Tear the leaves into bite-sized pieces, put into your salad bowl and spoon the potatoes and bacon over them.

5   Put your mustard vinaigrette into the still-warm frying pan, scrape up all the juices and pour this dressing over the potatoes and bacon.

★   *This is at its best if eaten while it's still warm.*

★ 23   GREEN BEANS, PANCETTA,   Serves 2
CHERVIL, WALNUT OIL

The secret is not to overcook the beans. You can cook them well in advance of making the salad. Once the beans are cooked, dunk them in very cold water to stop them cooking further. This way you'll know that they're perfect.

6–8 oz/170–225 g Kenyan or
    Bobby beans
1 or 2 Belgian endive
handful (1 oz/30 g) fresh chervil
1 tbsp fresh tarragon leaves
4 long or 2 circular slices of
    pancetta
1 tsp butter/olive oil
2 tbsp roughly chopped walnut
    halves

for the dressing:
$\frac{1}{2}$ tbsp red or white wine vinegar
2 tbsp walnut oil
sea salt
freshly ground black pepper

i   Top and tail the beans and rinse them thoroughly under the cold tap. If you have a vegetable steamer, steam the beans for exactly $2\frac{1}{2}$ minutes, or boil them in a little water for 2 minutes. In either case, don't add the beans until the water is boiling; start timing from the moment the beans hit the boiling water/steam. Drain and dunk in cold water. Drain again.

2   Cut the bottom from the endive(s), discard the few outer leaves, break off the crisp white leaves and slice them 2 or 3 times lengthways before putting them in your salad bowl along with the cooked beans.

3   Wash and spin dry the chervil, remove any thick stalks and add to the salad bowl.

4   Chop the tarragon leaves roughly and add to the salad bowl.

5   Trim the rind from the pancetta, and put it in a frying pan with a teaspoon of butter or olive oil. Fry for 1 or 2 minutes, then add the chopped walnut halves. Continue cooking until the pancetta has turned a deep colour and browned at the edges. Let everything cool for about 5 minutes, then make the dressing in the pan (vinegar first), scraping up all the juices with a wooden spoon.

6   Pour this over the leaves and beans in the salad bowl. Toss well and serve.

★   *For a more substantial salad you could crumble some strong tasting cheese – goat, Stilton or Roquefort – over the top in which case you might also add a teaspoon of Dijon mustard to the dressing.*

TUNA, BORLOTTI BEANS, SPRING ONIONS

Serves 2

This is best served on a bed of crispy Cos lettuce.

3 oz/ 85 g dried borlotti beans
or 7 oz/200 g tin of ready-cooked
    borlotti beans
1 tsp butter or olive oil
½ fresh unwaxed or organic lemon
sea salt

freshly ground black pepper
7 oz/200 g tin dolphin-friendly tuna
    steak
1 fresh Cos lettuce
6–8 spring onions
2 tbsp extra virgin olive oil
2 tbsp fresh basil leaves

1   Soak the dried borlotti beans overnight if you cannot find ready-cooked ones. Bring a saucepan of water to the boil, add the borlotti beans and cook over a medium heat for up to an hour. Drain the beans and return to the saucepan with a teaspoon of butter or olive oil, some freshly grated lemon zest, a pinch of sea salt and some freshly ground black pepper.

2   Drain the tuna from its cannig liquid, put it in a bowl and break it up with a fork. Squeeze most of the juice from the half lemon, and grind 2 or 3 turns of black pepper over the tuna.

3   Trim and wash the Cos, removing any very thick stalks and any discoloured or limp leaves. Spin it dry, then tear it into smallish pieces and put in your salad bowl.

4   Trim the spring onions and remove the outer layer of skin. Slice them lengthways into very fine strips and scatter these over the Cos leaves.

5   Scatter the borlotti beans and crumble the tuna over the salad.

6   Make the dressing with the remaining lemon juice, extra virgin olive oil, and roughly torn basil leaves.

7   Pour this over the salad and toss very gently, taking care not to create a mush with the tuna.

★   *Serve with warm crusty bread. Or, keeping the salad leaves separate, pile the tuna and borlotti beans on top of a piece of toast rubbed with fresh garlic and dribbled with olive oil and serve with a wedge of lemon to squeeze over the top.*

THE PERFECT LENTIL SALAD Serves 3–4

If you cook your lentils like this you won't ever be disappointed. You can eat them as a side dish with almost anything (particularly good with sausages and white fish such as cod or halibut) or add them to green or vegetable salads.

Cooked lentils will last for a couple of days in the fridge. They reheat well (you may need to add a little extra liquid) and are a delicious addition to soup. We think the dark Puy lentils are the best as they retain their 'bite' better than the flatter greener lentils, but green lentils will work just as well.

1 medium-sized fresh carrot	3 sage leaves
1 small onion	1 sprig each thyme and rosemary
1 stick celery	
1 clove of garlic	*for the dressing:*
4 cloves	1½ tbsp extra virgin olive oil
butter/olive oil for cooking	½ tbsp balsamic vinegar
5 oz/150 g Puy lentils	1 tsp Dijon mustard
½ pint/290 ml chicken or vegetable	sea salt
stock	freshly ground black pepper

1   Peel and grate the carrot. Peel and chop the onion very finely. Clean and chop the celery very finely. Peel and crush the garlic clove.

2   Put all the above, with the 4 cloves, into a saucepan with a large teaspoon of butter or olive oil. Fry gently until the onion and celery start to become translucent. Turn the heat up a bit, add the lentils and stir well so that they are coated with butter/oil. Add the stock, cover the pan and simmer for 15 minutes. Add the sage, thyme and rosemary. Cook for a further 5 minutes.

3   By this time most of the stock will have been absorbed. Remove the pan from the heat, keep the lid on and leave it to cool for 10 minutes.

4   If there seems to be a lot of liquid, drain some of it off. It's important that lentils have some liquid around them or they become dry and floury.

5   Remove the herbs and the cloves if you can find them just before serving.

6   Make the dressing and pour over the warm lentils.

★   *To complete the salad, chop some flat parsley leaves and scatter on top with some grated lemon zest, or fry some bacon cut into strips and stir into the lentils.*

Toasted walnuts and some crumbled goats' cheese scattered over the top also taste very good.

★ 26　ORIENTAL PRAWN, GINGER, Serves 2–3
SOY, SESAME, SPRING ONION,
SUGAR SNAP PEAS

This salad may seem complicated but please don't be put off – it's very easy to make and well worth it. If you prefer you can use chicken breast instead of prawns. Just cut the raw chicken into slim slices and cook for a little longer than you would the prawns.

lump of fresh root ginger the size
   of a walnut
plump firm clove of fresh garlic
1 fresh Dutch Red chilli pepper
2 tbsp lemon juice
8 oz/225 g large prawns, preferably
   uncooked
1 heaped tsp of fresh thyme leaves
3 tbsp soy sauce

sesame seeds – black and white
sea salt
freshly ground black pepper
8 oz/225 g fresh sugar snap peas
6–8 spring onions
3 tbsp sesame oil
red wine vinegar or rice wine
   vinegar if you can find it
1 tsp clear honey

1　Peel and chop or grate the ginger and the garlic very finely.

2　Top and tail the chilli pepper, remove the pith and seeds from the inside and chop very finely. You will need 2 teaspoons or so of chopped chilli.

3　Grate the zest from the half lemon.

4　Peel the prawns and put them in a bowl with the chopped garlic, ginger, chilli, lemon zest, 1 tablespoon of lemon juice, the thyme leaves, 2 tablespoons of soy sauce and a teaspoon of sesame seeds. Sprinkle a pinch of sea salt and a few grinds of black pepper.

5　Top and tail the sugar snap peas and rinse them under a running tap. Steam them for $2\frac{1}{2}$ minutes maximum and then dunk them in cold water to stop them cooking further.

6　Trim the spring onions, remove the outside layer of skin. Chop 1 or 2 of them into extremely fine circular slices and put these in your salad bowl. Chop the rest into wider slices cut on the diagonal and reserve.

7　Make the dressing in the salad bowl with the finely sliced spring onion. Add 1 tablespoon soy sauce, 1 tablespoon freshly squeezed lemon juice, 2 tablespoons of the sesame oil, 1 tablespoon vinegar, 1 teaspoon clear honey.

8　Add the sugar snap peas and toss in the dressing so they are well coated.

9   Heat I tablespoon of sesame oil in a frying pan until hot. Add the marinated prawns and all their juice and stir-fry briefly for I or 2 minutes (if you have a wok, so much the better). Make sure the prawns are being cooked on both sides and continue to stir-fry for another minute or two until the prawns are creamy white tinged with pink and starting to go golden brown at the edges. Add the reserved spring onions and stir them around so they become coated with the cooking juices.

10   Add everything from the pan to the sugar snap peas in the bowl and toss well. Scatter some more sesame seeds on top and serve. You can add a couple of handfuls of watercress at the last moment if you need some more greenery.

27

BACON AND EGG SALAD

This is in fact a classic French Brasserie salad. It is usually made with curly endive lettuce, called frisée, and those wonderful thick sticks of bacon called lardons. You can buy ready-prepared 'lardons' in packs from some supermarkets. The trick is poaching the eggs. If you are worried about this, simply soft boil the eggs (3 minutes) and peel them carefully in cold water so that the shell comes away easily without tearing the egg.

Otherwise follow our instructions and you'll be delighted with how easy it is. This is a terrific salad: either as a starter or as a light supper.

1 head of curly endive lettuce	*for the dressing:*
1 tsp white wine vinegar	1 tbsp chopped chives
2 size-2 free-range eggs – organic if possible	1 tsp Dijon mustard
	1 ½ tbsp extra virgin olive oil
4 slices bacon or pancetta cut really thick (¼ in/ ½ cm)	1 tbsp sunflower oil
	2 tsp red or white wine vinegar
	sea salt
	freshly ground black pepper

1 Trim and wash the lettuce thoroughly in cold water. Don't use the darker green outside leaves as they can be bitter. Spin dry or roll in a tea towel, tear the leaves into bite-sized pieces and put them in your salad bowl.

2 Put all the ingredients for the salad dressing in a small bowl or mug and whisk together with a fork.

3 *Poaching the eggs:* fill a small saucepan three quarters full with water. Bring to the boil. Add 1 teaspoon white wine vinegar. Whisk the water with a fork or whisk until a whirlpool is formed. Break the eggs, one after another, into the centre of the whirlpool (you may need to continue stirring around the edge of the pan – always in the same direction, of course – to keep the current going). Turn off the heat, cover the saucepan and poach for exactly 3 minutes, timed from when the egg hits the water. Remove with a slotted spoon (a large metal spoon with holes in it) and drain on some kitchen towel.

★ Remember – THE FRESHER THE EGGS, THE BETTER THEY WILL POACH.

4   While the eggs are poaching remove the rind from the bacon and chop into thick matchstick shapes using a pair of scissors. Dry-fry the bacon over a medium heat until it is well browned. Scatter the hot bacon pieces over the salad leaves. Put the poached eggs on top. Add the dressing to the hot frying pan, let it sizzle for a few seconds, then pour it over the eggs and bacon and serve immediately.

★   *You could add some buttered toast, cut into $\frac{1}{2}$ in/1 cm squares, to the bacon pieces halfway through cooking (perhaps adding a teaspoon of sunflower oil if necessary) and fry them with the bacon, making delicious bacony croûtons and ending up with a* **Bacon, Egg and Toast Salad.**

28

SALAD NIÇOISE

This is one of our all-time favourite summer salads. When tomatoes are in season and really sweet and juicy beans and lettuce also are at their best, make this salad and eat it outside if possible – it's one of the greats. This recipe will satisfy 2 very hungry people, or serve 4 as a starter or light lunch.

3 or 4 egg-sized new potatoes
6 oz/170 g fresh green beans
1 large Cos lettuce
6–8 medium-sized vine-ripened
   tomatoes
7 oz/200 g tin dolphin-friendly tuna
2 freshly hard-boiled eggs
4 anchovy fillets
2 heaped tbsp black olives
2 tbsp fresh flat parsley leaves,
   roughly chopped

for the dressing:
1 fresh garlic clove, peeled,
   crushed, and finely chopped
1 tsp fresh thyme leaves
small bunch fresh chervil, stalks
   removed, roughly chopped
1 tsp Dijon mustard
2 tbsp extra virgin olive oil
2 tbsp sunflower oil
1 tsp red wine vinegar
1 tbsp freshly squeezed lemon juice
1 tsp freshly grated lemon zest
sea salt
freshly ground black pepper

1   Put all the dressing ingredients into a bowl/mug/jar and whisk together using a fork.

2   Cook the potatoes in plenty of boiling water for 20–25 minutes. Drain. When cool enough to handle, peel off the skins and slice the potatoes no thicker than ¼ in/½ cm. Put these in your salad bowl.

3   Top and tail the green beans. Rinse them under a cold tap. Steam or boil them in a little water for exactly 2½ minutes. Dunk them in cold water to stop them cooking further. Drain well and add to the potatoes.

4   Trim and wash the Cos thoroughly. Spin dry or roll in a tea towel. Tear into bite-sized pieces and put into your salad bowl.

5   Pour half of the dressing over the lettuce, beans and potatoes and toss, using your hands so that the potato slices don't disintegrate.

6   Wash and wipe dry the tomatoes. You can peel them if you feel like it (immerse them in boiling water for 30 seconds, cool under a running tap, slip the skins off). Slice them across their width and arrange these slices over the tossed lettuce, etc, in the salad bowl.

7   Drain the tuna from the tin and crumble it over the tomato slices in the bowl.

8   Peel the eggs and slice each one lengthways into 6 segments. Arrange these segments amongst the tuna.

9   Cut each anchovy fillet in half lengthways and criss-cross over the eggs and tuna.

10   Remove the stones from the olives by tearing them in half if they're soft enough (*see page 15 for notes on olives*). Scatter the olive halves over the salad.

11   Shake the rest of the dressing over the salad.

12   Scatter the flat parsley leaves, a pinch of sea salt and a few grinds of black pepper on top.

★   *Serve with warm French bread – baguette – and unsalted butter.*

29

CAESAR SALAD

Serves 2

Don't be put off by the strong combination of garlic, parmesan and anchovy. This salad is a classic invented by a restauranteur called Caesar Cardini during the 1920s in Tijuana, Mexico. Here's our version for which you will need impeccably fresh free-range eggs, good quality Parmesan (parmigiano-reggiano) and well-made croûtons.

1 fresh Cos or Sweet Romaine lettuce
6–8 thin ($\frac{1}{4}$ in/$\frac{1}{2}$ cm) slices of baguette (sliced multigrain bread is good too – 2 slices)
1 clove fresh garlic
2 tbsp olive oil
2 heaped tbsp freshly shaved Parmesan

for the dressing:
1 fresh plump clove garlic, peeled and crushed
sea salt
2 anchovy fillets
1 fresh free-range egg yolk
2 tsp Worcester sauce
1 tbsp lemon juice
freshly ground pepper
2 tbsp extra virgin olive oil
2 heaped tbsp freshly grated Parmesan
1 tbsp mayonnaise

1   Put all the ingredients for the dressing in a mini-blender and whizz for two minutes. If you are making the dressing by hand, make it in the bottom of the salad bowl. Squeeze the garlic through a press, then add a small pinch of sea salt and pound the salt and garlic together with a wooden spoon. Chop the anchovy fillets as finely as you can with scissors and pound into the garlic. (Anchovy fillets disintegrate very quickly so it won't take long.) Add the egg yolk, Worcester sauce, fresh lemon juice, a few grinds of black pepper, and whisk together with a fork. Add the olive oil, a little at a time, whisking all the while, then add the grated Parmesan and continue to whisk until the dressing is thick and creamy. Finally add the mayonnaise and whisk in.

2   Trim and wash the Cos lettuce thoroughly, taking care to remove any thick stalks. Spin dry or roll dry in a tea towel. Tear into bite-sized pieces and put into your salad bowl (over the dressing if it's hand-made, but do not toss the salad).

3   Toast the slices of baguette or bread very lighty. Let them cool a little, then rub them with a peeled garlic clove. Put them in a baking tray or dish, brush or dribble olive oil over both sides and put them in a preheated oven, 190°C/375°F/Gas mark 5, for 10 minutes. No longer or they will bake hard and crack your teeth. When they're cool enough to handle, cut the baguette slices into rough quarters, or the granary slices into $\frac{1}{2}$ in/1 cm squares and scatter them over the Cos leaves in the salad bowl.

4   Pour the dressing over the leaves and croutons if it's not already in the bowl and toss well so that everything is thoroughly coated.

5   Scatter the shaved Parmesan over the top and serve immediately.

30

PRET'S VERSION OF THE CHEF'S SALAD

Serves 2–3

This must have been invented as a way of using leftovers. Whether you use leftovers or get the ingredients specially, this is a great lunch-time salad. We suggest using a mix of salad leaves, but you could stick to Cos alone.

1 handful Cos lettuce leaves
1 handful radicchio leaves
1 handful watercress
2–3 oz/55–85 g honey roast ham
1 freshly cooked chicken breast
2–3 oz/55–85 g Gruyère or
   Emmenthal cheese
2 freshly hard-boiled eggs
2 medium-sized tomatoes

for the dressing:
1 teaspoon Dijon mustard
$1\frac{1}{2}$ tbsp extra virgin olive oil
1 tbsp sunflower oil
1 tbsp mayonnaise
2 tsp red or white wine vinegar
sea salt
freshly ground black pepper

1   Wash and dry the lettuce thoroughly. Tear the leaves into bite-sized pieces and put into your salad bowl. Toss together to mix the different leaves.
2   Whisk together all the dressing ingredients in a bowl and, just before serving, add most of the dressing to the salad leaves and toss well.
3   Slice the ham, chicken and cheese into similarly sized strips, about $\frac{1}{4}$ in/$\frac{1}{2}$ cm wide and 3–4 cm long. Scatter these over the dressed salad leaves.
4   Peel the hard-boiled eggs, and cut them into quarters.
5   Wash and dry the tomatoes and cut them into quarters.
6   Arrange the egg and tomato quarters over the salad.
7   Pour the rest of the dressing over the meat, cheese and eggs and serve.

★   *You could try adding a tablespoon of fresh tarragon leaves, roughly chopped, to the dressing to give a slightly different and extremely delicious touch.*

★ 31   BACON AND AVOCADO   Serves 2
WITH MUSTARD DRESSING

Very simple, very good. An ideal starter, or main salad served with a baked potato.

2 large handfuls of mixed salad
   leaves: Cos, radiccio, rocket,
   curly endive
1 perfectly ripe avocado
bunch of fresh chervil or basil
8–10 rashers streaky bacon

for the dressing:
1 tsp Dijon mustard
1 tbsp balsamic vinegar
sea salt
freshly ground black pepper
3 tbsp extra virgin olive oil

1   Wash the salad leaves thoroughly and spin dry. Remove any thick stalks and any discoloured or limp leaves. Tear into bite-sized pieces. Put into your salad bowl.

2   Peel the avocado and remove the stone. Place each half cut side down and slice crosswise at an angle. Strew the pieces of avocado over the lettuce.

3   Wash and dry the chervil or basil. Remove any large stalks. Tear the chervil into smaller pieces or tear the basil leaves in half and scatter over the salad.

4   *The dressing:* combine the mustard and balsamic vinegar in a bowl with a small pinch of sea salt and a few grinds of black pepper. Whisk in the olive oil.

5   Remove the bacon rind. Dry-fry the bacon for 2–3 minutes on each side, so that it is just becoming crispy. You don't want it too crispy or the texture will be unpleasant in the salad. Using scissors, snip the rashers into ½ in/1 cm-wide strips, cutting at an angle, and scatter these over the salad. While the frying pan is still hot, add the mustard dressing, let it sizzle for a few seconds, then scrape all the juices together and pour over the salad.

6   Toss gently, so the avocado slices don't disintegrate and serve immediately while the bacon is still warm.

★   *Before dry-frying the bacon, you could snip it into ½ in/1 cm strips, and fry it ready-cut. Halfway through cooking add 2 tablespoons of pinenuts or chopped walnuts and brown them with the bacon for an extra nutty taste. Crumble some goats' cheese or feta over the salad just before serving.*

★ 32 **MOZZARELLA, PLUM TOMATO, AVOCADO, BASIL** Serves 2

The classic Italian restaurant starter. Made at home with impeccably fresh good-quality ingredients it will taste a good deal better than something which costs you four times as much in a second-rate restaurant. You can make it on a bed of finely shredded radicchio tossed in some fresh lemon juice and extra virgin olive oil. We think this salad looks best untossed, with the dressing spooned over the top and served in a shallow dish or on a brightly coloured plate.

2 plum tomatoes
1 perfectly ripe avocado
sea salt
1 fresh mozzarella ball, preferably
    buffalo mozzarella
freshly ground black pepper
3 tbsp fresh basil leaves

for the dressing:
1 tbsp freshly squeezed lemon juice
or
1 tbsp balsamic vinegar
3–4 tbsp extra virgin olive oil

1   Cut a tiny cross at the bottom of each tomato and immerse the tomatoes in boiling water for 30 seconds. Drain and cool under a running tap. Remove the stalks and slide off the skins. Slice each tomato in half lengthways. Slice each half again, lengthways. Chop these quarters into $\frac{1}{2}$ in/1 cm-wide pieces. Arrange them over the plate.

2   Cut the avocado in half, remove the stone and peel. Place each half cut side down, slice lengthways into 3 or 4 segments, then slice crossways at an angle into $\frac{1}{2}$ in/1 cm-wide pieces. Strew these over the chopped tomatoes.

3   Scatter a pinch of sea salt over the tomatoes and avocado.

4   Remove the mozzarella from its bag and squeeze it gently in your hand to drain it. Slice it into $\frac{1}{4}$ in/$\frac{1}{2}$ cm-wide slices and cut each slice into 3 or 4 strips. Scatter these over the tomatoes and avocado.

5   Grind some black pepper over the salad.

6   Wash and dry the basil leaves. Tear them into strips and scatter over the salad.

7   Whisk the lemon juice/vinegar and oil together in a bowl and spoon carefully over the salad so that everything is covered.

★   *Serve with a crusty bread such as Ciabatta and perhaps some tapenade (see page 125).*

MOZZARELLA   In Italy, the home of mozzarella, 2 or 3-day-old cheese is considered past it. The mozzarella cheeses made for export last for about 2 weeks, so when you are buying mozzarella check its expiry date. If it is only a few days away, it means the cheese is nearing the end of its life and you should avoid it. Buy mozzarellas which have at least two weeks' grace. Buffalo mozzarella (*mozzarella di bufalo*) is considered the best, and this is reflected in its price. It is wonderful as long as it is fresh as can be. Otherwise the large supermarkets (Sainsbury's and Waitrose in particular) have a good cowsmilk mozzarella which is reasonably priced and tastes fresh and delicate.

Mozzarella is stored in milky water, and sometimes wrapped in paper first. It should be creamy white in colour and taste clean and fresh. If it tastes fizzy and is within its sell-by date take it back to your supplier and complain. Don't ever buy the 'pizza topping' mozzarella vacuum packed in plastic – it is a pale yellowy colour and just like rubber.

★ 33 **GRILLED GOATS' CHEESE** Serves 2
WITH MESCLUN

Mesclun is the name given to a particular mix of young salad leaves and herbs sold in France and across the Mediterranean. Most supermarkets sell ready-prepared bags of herb salad mix. If you want to make your own authentic mix we've listed the leaves you will need.

This is a wonderfully delicious and impressive starter or light lunch/supper.

2 large handfuls of mesclun: rocket, lambs leaf, oak leaf, curly endive, baby Cos, radicchio, sprigs of chervil and flat-leaf parsley
sea salt
2 tbsp walnut pieces
2 small round goats' cheeses, or a large one cut in half
I heaped tbsp chopped chives

for the dressing:
$\frac{1}{2}$ tsp Dijon mustard
I tbsp balsamic vinegar
freshly ground black pepper
I tbsp extra virgin olive oil
3 tbsp walnut oil

I Wash the mesclun thoroughly. Remove any thick stalks and discoloured or limp leaves. Tear any larger leaves into smaller pieces – this salad mix should be composed of young, small tender leaves. Spin dry and put into your salad bowl. Scatter a pinch of sea salt over the leaves.

2 Pick out any bits of dried membrane from the walnut pieces, then scatter them over the salad leaves.

3 Whisk the mustard and balsamic vinegar together in a bowl with some freshly ground black pepper, then add the oils and whisk everything together. Pour most of this over the salad and walnuts and toss thoroughly.

4 Put the goats' cheese rounds on some silver foil on a grill tray and place about 2–2$\frac{1}{2}$ in/5–6 cm under a preheated medium grill for about 5 minutes. Watch them carefully; you want the tops to brown and bubble but not burn.

5 Divide the salad between 2 plates and top with the grilled goats' cheese. Spoon dressing over each cheese and sprinkle on chopped chives. Serve at once.

★ *Make this more substantial by toasting two slices of walnut bread, and brushing them with olive oil. Sit the grilled goats' cheese on top of the toast and arrange the salad around it or simply crumble some goats' cheese over the dressed salad and serve with crusty bread.*

Anyone who has been to Greece or Cyprus will have eaten this. We think our version measures up pretty well. Feta, ricotta salata, or Halloumi cheese are all perfect for this salad.

4 oz/110 g feta cheese
½ cucumber
4 medium perfectly ripe tomatoes
1 small red onion
2½ oz/75 g marinated black olives
   (see page 15)
1 tbsp fresh mint and/or marjoram
   leaves
1 unwaxed or organic lemon

for the dressing:
juice of ½ lemon
3 tbsp extra virgin olive oil
   (preferably Greek)
1 tbsp balsamic vinegar
freshly ground black pepper

1 Cut the cheese into crumbly ½ in/1 cm cubes. Place in shallow dish or bowl.

2 Peel the half cucumber with a potato peeler and cut into rough cubes. Add to the cheese.

3 Wash and dry the tomatoes, remove their stalks, chop roughly and add to the bowl.

4 Peel the outside skin from the onion, cut into very fine segments and add them to the bowl.

5 Stone the olives by tearing them in half and squeezing out the stones. Add the torn olives to the bowl.

6 Tear the mint and/or marjoram leaves in half and scatter them over everything in the bowl.

7 Scrub the lemon under the cold tap and dry thoroughly. Cut the tail end off, then cut 4 slices, approx. ¼ in/½ cm wide. Cut these round slices into 6 or 8 small segments and add to the salad. Squeeze the juice from the remaining half lemon over the salad, catching the pips in a tea-strainer.

8 Pour 3 tablespoons of olive oil and 1 tablespoon of balsamic vinegar directly over the salad, then grind fresh black pepper generously over the salad.

9 Using your hands or 2 spoons gently combine all the ingredients so they are attractively mixed and well dressed, but be careful not to mush the cheese.

★ *This salad can be left to stand for half an hour or so at room temperature before you eat it. Serve with hot pitta bread, or any sort of rustic bread.*

COTTAGE CHEESE, BROCCOLI, BLACK OLIVES

Serves 2

You can substitute fresh ricotta cheese for the cottage cheese. This salad is quite garlicky, so use only a half clove of garlic if you're nervous.

6–8 oz/170–225 g fresh broccoli
2½ oz/75 g black olives, marinated in herbs and olive oil (see *page 15*)
4 oz/110 g cottage cheese

for the dressing:
1 fresh firm clove pink garlic
2 tbsp extra virgin olive oil
1 tbsp sunflower oil
1 tbsp balsamic vinegar
sea salt
freshly ground black pepper

1   If you can, make the dressing a few hours in advance so that the garlic has time to flavour the dressing fully. Peel and crush the garlic clove, chop finely or squeeze through a garlic press. Put it in a jam jar. Add the other dressing ingredients, screw on the lid and shake everything together.

2   Cut the florets of broccoli from the stalk and divide the larger florets so that they are bite-sized. Steam or boil them for 2 minutes. (Don't add the broccoli until the water is boiling – time from the moment the broccoli hits the boiling water/steam.) Drain and place in a salad bowl.

3   Tear the black olives in half and squeeze out the stones. Save 10 or so olive halves and add the rest to the broccoli.

4   Add the cottage cheese to the salad bowl, shake the dressing over the top, toss everything together and serve with the remaining olives scattered on top.

RICOTTA AND FETA, TOMATOES, PUMPKIN SEEDS

Serves 2

Mix these two crumbly cheeses (one mild, one strong) with summer tomatoes and hot pumpkin seeds and you have a slightly unusual but wonderfully balanced starter or light supper.

8 oz/225 g tomatoes (try to find
   small, vine-ripened tomatoes)
2 oz/55 g ricotta cheese
2 oz/55 g feta cheese
15 fresh basil leaves or small bunch
   of chervil
1 tsp olive oil
small pinch Herbes de Provence
2 tbsp pumpkin seeds (available
   from most supermarkets and
   health food shops)

for the dressing:
1 tbsp balsamic vinegar
3 tbsp extra virgin olive oil
freshly ground black pepper
sea salt (optional)

1 Wash and wipe dry the tomatoes. Remove the stalks. Chop them into quarters and if the tomatoes are larger than a golf ball, divide the quarters in half again. Arrange them on a large plate or shallow serving dish.

2 Chop the two cheeses into small cubes and drop them on top of the tomatoes, crumbling the cheese slightly with your fingers (you'll find it will crumble as you are cutting it anyway).

3 Tear the basil leaves into strips and scatter on top of the cheese and tomatoes. If using chervil, remove the stalky bit and scatter likewise.

4 Heat a teaspoon of ordinary olive oil in a saucepan, add a small pinch of Herbes de Provence and the pumpkin seeds. As the oil heats up the seeds will start to swell and jump about like popping corn – you must use a lid on the saucepan! Holding the lid firmly on the pan, shake it around for a few minutes on the heat so that the seeds are evenly browned (be careful of flying seeds when you look in). Pour the hot seeds evenly over the salad.

5 Spoon the balsamic vinegar and olive oil directly over the cheese and tomatoes. Grind some black pepper over the top.

6 There is no salt in this recipe as feta is pretty salty. If you do need more, scatter a pinch of Maldon sea salt over the salad after you have dressed it.

★ 37   **PARMESAN, ROCKET, FENNEL,**   Serves 2
WITH A LEMON DRESSING

If you can't find good Parmesan (Parmigiano-Reggiano) try using pecorino romano. This salad is a great accompaniment for red meat and fish as well as being extremely delicious on its own.

2 handfuls (approx. 2 oz/55 g) fresh
    rocket
1 medium-sized fresh firm fennel
    bulb
pinch sea salt
2 heaped tbsp shaved Parmesan or
    pecorino (approx 1 oz/30 g)

for the dressing:
1 tsp freshly grated lemon zest
1 tbsp freshly squeezed lemon juice
2 tbsp extra virgin olive oil
sea salt
freshly ground black pepper

1   Wash the rocket, pinch off any thick stalks and remove any discoloured or limp leaves. Spin dry and put them into your salad bowl.

2   Cut the top stalks from the fennel bulb, cut off the bottom and remove the outer layer of flesh. Cut the trimmed bulb in half top to bottom and cut out the thick core at the base. Place each half bulb cut side down and slice crossways very finely. Scatter these slices over the rocket.

3   Scatter a pinch of sea salt over the rocket and fennel.

4   Whisk together the dressing ingredients in a bowl and pour over the rocket and fennel. Toss using your hands so that the rocket leaves don't get bruised.

5   Scatter the Parmesan or pecorino shavings over the top and serve.

FENNEL   When buying raw fennel, look out for bulbs which have a pearly white glow – this is a sign of firm and juicy flesh. They should feel heavy for their size, be very firm to the touch and any fronds on the stalk should be a healthy green.

★ 38 STILTON, PEAR, WALNUT, Serves 2–3
RADICCHIO WITH A CREAMY DRESSING

Make sure your pear (we think Comice and Conference taste the best) is perfectly ripe so that its sweet juiciness balances the strong taste of the Stilton. If you can't get any Stilton, use Roquefort; but reduce the amount to 3 oz/85 g because it has a stronger sharper taste.

1 small head fresh radicchio	*for the dressing:*
pinch sea salt	1 oz/30 g Stilton, crumbled
1 tsp balsamic vinegar	1 tbsp balsamic vinegar
2 tsp olive oil	1 tbsp fromage frais
1 large perfectly ripe Comice pear	3 tbsp walnut oil
4 oz/110 g Stilton rind removed	freshly ground black pepper
2 tbsp walnut pieces	1–2 tsp milk (optional)
	1 tbsp fresh tarragon leaves, roughly chopped

1 Peel the outer 3 or 4 leaves from the radicchio. Cut it in half and cut out the tough white core at the base. Put each half cut side down and slice very finely so that you end up with shredded ribbons of radicchio. Put these into a salad bowl with a pinch of sea salt, 1 teaspoon of balsamic vinegar and 2 teaspoons olive oil. Toss thoroughly using your hands.
2 Unless the pear is organic, it is best to peel it. Use a very sharp knife or a potato peeler and be careful not to peel away much flesh with the skin. Cut into quarters and cut out the seeds and core. Cut each quarter crossways at an angle into pieces no wider than ¼ in/½ cm and scatter the pieces over the radicchio.
3 Trim any rind from the Stilton. Break and crumble 4 oz of Stilton into pieces roughly the size of the pear pieces or shave it against the slicing section on a grater. Scatter these over the salad along with the walnut pieces.
4 *The dressing:* mash 1 oz crumbled Stilton into the balsamic vinegar using a fork. Add the fromage frais, the walnut oil and some freshly ground black pepper. If the dressing seems too thick, you can thin it with a teaspoon or two of milk. Add the tarragon leaves, whisk again and spoon over the salad so that everything is covered.

★ *If you want to make life very luxurious, add some freshly cooked bacon while it's still warm and/or some smoked turkey, which is a wonderful combination.*

FENNEL, TARRAGON, BROAD BEANS WITH A WALNUT DRESSING

Serves 2

This is deliciously fresh and light and is best when broad beans are in season at the beginning of the summer.

1 lb/475 g broad beans in their pods
or 6–8 oz/170–225 g tinned/ frozen broad beans
1 tsp walnut oil
1 medium-sized fresh firm fennel bulb
2 tbsp fresh tarragon leaves, thoroughly washed and drained

for the dressing:
1 tsp poppy seeds
1 tbsp natural live yoghurt
1 tbsp freshly squeezed lemon juice
2 tbsp walnut oil
sea salt
freshly ground black pepper

1 Remove the broad beans from their pods and peel away their waxy skins so that you are left with bright green and tender beans. Steam these for 1 minute, remove from the pan and put in a shallow dish. Add a teaspoon of walnut oil and stir the beans about so that they're well coated.

2 Cut the stalks from the top of the fennel bulb. Cut off the bottom and remove the outer layer of flesh. Cut in half lengthways and break the thick fleshy layers away from the core. Slice each of these lengthways into thin strips, no wider than $\frac{1}{8}$ in/$\frac{1}{4}$ cm and scatter them over the broad beans.

3 Chop the fresh tarragon leaves once or twice and scatter over the fennel and broad beans.

4 Whisk the ingredients for the dressing together in a bowl, pour over the salad and toss gently so you don't break up the broad beans.

★ *This is particularly good served alongside hot or cold salmon. Or you could cut some slices of smoked salmon into long thin strips like pappardelle and combine them gently with the salad, scattering a few fennel seeds and some torn chervil on top.*

Part Two

PRET

THE SANDWICHES

★

★ THE SANDWICHES ★

1 **Egg Mayonnaise and Bacon** 75

2 **Avocado and Prawn** 78

3 **Ham and Dijon Mustard Mayonnaise** 80

4 **Tuna Mayonnaise, Cucumber and Rocket** 82

5 **Chicken Breast, Avocado, Chargrilled Red Peppers, Salsa Verde** 84

6 **Spicy Chicken, Yoghurt, Mint Mayo, Watercress** 86

7 **Pret's Vegetarian Club with Fresh Herb Mayo** 88

8 **Goats' Cheese, Pink Peppercorns, Tomato, Rocket** 90

9 **Smoked Salmon, Cream Cheese, Dill and Mustard Sauce, Watercress** 92

10 **Chicken and Bacon Club** 94

11 **Prawns, Tomato and Parsley** 95

12 **Smoked Salmon Deluxe** 96

13 **Poached Salmon and Watercress** 97

14 **Pret's All-Day Breakfast** 100

15 **Mature Cheddar with Fruit Chutney** 101

16 **Pastrami and Dill Pickle on Rye** 102

17 **Smoked Salmon Tartare, Spring Onions, Capers, Tarragon and Sour Cream** 104

18 **Ham, Cream Cheese, Tomato, Mustard, Lettuce** 106

19 **Smoked Trout or Mackerel, Horseradish Mayo, Watercress** 107

20 **Crunchy Peanut Butter, Redcurrant Jelly, Banana** 108

21 **Roast Turkey, Cranberry Sauce, Pinenuts, Watercress** 109

22 **Avocado, Mozzarella, Tomato, Roast Fennel, Pinenuts, Fresh Basil** 110

23 **Lamb, Redcurrant Jelly, Chargrilled Aubergine** 112

24 **Ricotta, Chargrilled Aubergine, Tomato, Walnut** 114

THE SANDWICHES

25 **Feta, Red Onion, Yoghurt and Mint Dressing** 116

26 **Chicken and Tarragon, with Tomato and Salad** 117

27 **Smoked Mackerel, Fresh Dill Cucumber, Tomato** 118

28 **Smoked Salmon and Fresh Dill Cucumber** 120

29 **Bacon and Avocado** 121

30 **Stilton, Crispy Bacon, Red Grapes, Walnuts, Fromage Frais** 122

31 **Chicken, Orange, Black Olives or Tapenade with Rocket** 124

32 **Ricotta or Cottage Cheese, Pesto, Tomato and Rocket** 126

33 **Salami, Ricotta, Red Onion, Tomato, Black Olives** 128

34 **Roast Beef, Mustard and Horseradish Sauce, Rocket and Tomato** 130

35 **Roast Beef, Balsamic Vinegar-Soaked Rocket, Cream Cheese** 132

All of these sandwiches can be made using ingredients from supermarkets and delis. In the cases of chargrilled vegetables, roast or baked vegetables, marinated olives, cooked chicken breasts, etc, we've included recipes for how to do these at home if you're keen to prepare everything yourself because they are quick and easy and take very little extra time. And if you follow our recipes they *will* taste better than if they came straight from a supermarket.

Since we opened our first shop in 1986 we have sold millions of sandwiches. We try to move with the times and please our customers by introducing new lines and redefining and improving old ones. One thing hasn't changed and that is the undisputed popularity and wonderful convenience of the sandwich. In fact the status of the sandwich seems to go up and up. Whether you are making a packed lunch to take to work, a picnic, a quick snack to eat in front of the TV, or a square meal, the sandwich fits all bills.

THE BREAD   There are hundreds of different kinds of bread around these days. Which one should you use? The answer is any one – whatever you've got – as long as it's FRESH! Some of our recipes recommend a particular type of bread, but most of them leave that part up to you. **PRET A MANGER** has always avoided the mass-produced white loaf. We much prefer the malted brown, walnut, tomato, and other savoury breads which are now easily available everywhere.

THE FILLING   Remember that a sandwich will only ever be as good as the quality of its ingredients. However skilful you are, a sandwich made from dry bread, limp lettuce, sour tomatoes and slimy ham will never make it. It is vital that you use really fresh ingredients.

We think it is important to season seandwiches with a little sea salt or herb salt and freshly ground black pepper. How much you use is up to you.

Some of our recipes suggest you use butter (usually unsalted so that all the other wonderful tastes come through) but again this is a personal thing. Remember to let butter warm to room temperature before you use it or it will tear the bread. If you are slicing your own loaf, butter the slice before you cut it from the loaf.

Tomatoes and lettuce feature a lot in our recipes. A perfectly ripe tomato which has plenty of flavour yet still retains a slightly acidic bite is an unbeatable ingredient in sandwich-making. Likewise, a fresh crisp lettuce gives a sandwich a wonderful crunch – important when the majority of other ingredients are soft and smooth. Look out for vine-ripened tomatoes in the supermarkets and greengrocers, they certainly have more flavour than many of the obviously underripe tomatoes on offer. Beef tomatoes (as long as they are deep red and heavy for their size) are sweeter and juicier than regular tomatoes. We have indicated where we think it's worth using them.

The bags of ready-prepared salad leaves, sold in supermarkets, are convenient and easy to use for sandwiches. (Please see pages 5–7 for notes on salad leaves.)

WRAPPING   Whether you're making a daily lunchbox sandwich or a selection to take on a picnic, your sandwiches must arrive in good condition. You should therefore:

1   Use thick slices of bread so the filling doesn't soak through.
2   Keep them cool (in the fridge until you set off).
3   Wrap them in greaseproof paper, labelling them if necessary. Don't use clingfilm, which makes sandwiches sweat.
4   Pack them carefully so they won't be squashed.

AND FINALLY...
★   If possible, don't slice sandwiches in half until just before you eat them. The bread will protect the filling up to the last minute and the sandwich will taste fresher and juicier.
★   If you take a sandwich from the fridge, let it warm to room temperature before you bite into it. It will taste better.

★ 1   EGG MAYONNAISE AND BACON   Serves 1

Nothing beats freshly fried egg and bacon, hot from the pan, put between two slices of toasted bread, but this is something that can be eaten only at home. Our version will travel, and as long as the bacon is good quality, will stay good for most of the day. Obviously, to make a really good egg and bacon sandwich, you've got to have excellent egg mayo and impeccably crispy bacon.

2 slices fresh bread, buttered if you like
1 heaped tbsp egg mayonnaise (see p. 76)
4–5 rashers streaky bacon, rinds removed

3–4 slices beef tomato
seasoning: sea salt or herb salt and freshly ground black pepper
small handful (approx. ½ oz/15 g) mixed lettuce

Preparing the filling:

1 Dry fry the bacon (see p. 76) over a medium heat until it's just crispy, then remove from the pan and place on some crumpled-up kitchen towel which will absorb any extra fat.
2 Wash and wipe dry the beef tomato. Remember to remove the stalk and cut out any tough white core from the stalk end. Slice the tomato across its width into slices not wider than ¼ in/½ cm.
3 Wash the lettuce and either spin dry or roll gently in a tea towel.
4 The bacon will now be cool enough to handle. Break it into pieces (the more it has been cooked – the crispier it is – the easier it will break and crumble).

Assembling the sandwich:

1 Spread 1 heaped tbsp egg mayonnaise on bottom slice of bread.
2 Scatter the bacon evenly over the egg mayo.
3 Arrange 3 or 4 slices of beef tomato to cover the egg mayo and bacon.
4 Season.
5 Cover with lettuce.
6 Top with the second slice of bread, press down gently but firmly and slice in half.

Best ever Egg Mayonnaise

Try to buy free-range eggs. (We use Martin Pitt's free-range eggs – available in health food shops and speciality food shops.) All supermarkets stock free-range eggs and they do taste better.

4 size-2 free-range eggs, boiled for 6 minutes
1 tbsp butter
herb salt

freshly ground black pepper
1–2 tbsp mayonnaise
small pinch mild curry powder

1 Shell the hot eggs under a running cold tap. Shake off the water and put them in a clean dry bowl. Add the butter, a pinch of herb salt and some freshly ground black pepper and mash everything together with a fork. Don't over-mash, it's important that the egg mayo is chunky. Let it cool for 10 minutes or so. Then add the mayonnaise, and a small pinch of mild curry powder and stir together.

★ *This makes enough egg mayo for 2 large rounds of sandwiches.*
For a reduced calorie version, skip the butter and use low-cal mayo.

BACON We think that streaky bacon (from the pork belly) is best for sandwiches and salads. We choose a mild (i.e. not very smoky or salty) streaky bacon. If you can find dry cured bacon – which hasn't had water and brine injected into it during the curing process – use it. It tastes better, crisps better, and isn't full of unwanted additives and preservatives. Trim off the rind with a pair of scissors before you cook the bacon. We find that rind can be tough and chewy in sandwiches.

If you buy bacon which is sliced for you, make sure it is sliced *thin*, $\frac{1}{8}$ in/ 1–2 mm. The thinner it's sliced, the better it crisps.

Dry frying: This is the best way to cook streaky bacon – in its own fat. However, if the bacon is very lean (i.e. very thin streaks of fat, or almost none at all) you will need to cook it in a teaspoon of butter. Let's assume you've found perfect streaky bacon with a good proportion of meat to fat, say 60/40. Lay the rashers in your non-stick frying pan, and cook on a low to medium heat until the fat starts to run. Move the rashers about so that they don't stick to the pan, turn the heat up to medium and leave them for about 4 minutes. Turn them over and leave them for a further 5 or so minutes by which time they should be starting to crisp. Let them crisp for another minute or two, then remove them from the pan and place on crumpled kitchen paper to drain. Don't leave bacon to cool down in the pan, it will quickly become soggy and eventually chewy.

Grilling: Put some kitchen foil in your grillpan (saves you washing up), lay the rashers of streaky bacon on the wire rack and grill for 3–4 minutes $1\frac{1}{2}$–2 in/4–5 cm below a preheated medium grill, then turn the rashers over and do the same on the other side. They should be nicely crisp by now. If not, keep grilling for another few minutes.

If you're very hungry, spread some bread or toast with a little butter and orange marmalade, add the freshly cooked bacon, cover with more buttered bread or toast and eat immediately. Yum.

AVOCADO AND PRAWN   Serves 1

(secretly) love Marie Rose sauce which is probably why this
one of our bestsellers. Try it on wholegrain or rye bread.

2 slices fresh bread, buttered if you
   like
½ perfectly ripe avocado
1 tbsp Marie Rose sauce (see
   opposite)
small handful (2–3 oz/55–85 g)
   defrosted prawns

¼ fresh lemon
small pinch paprika
seasoning: sea salt/herb salt, freshly
   ground black pepper
crisp green lettuce such as Cos:
   3 or 4 medium-sized leaves

Preparing the filling:

1   Cut the avocado in half top to bottom. Peel the stoneless half, lay it face
down on the chopping surface and slice into ¼ in/½ cm slices, cutting
lengthways. (The remaining half can be stored in the fridge for a day or two –
leave the stone in place, squeeze some fresh lemon juice over the flesh, wrap
tightly in clingfilm.)
2   Drain the prawns well, place in a small bowl and squeeze some fresh
lemon juice over them using a tea-strainer to catch the lemon pips. Sprinkle
the paprika over the prawns.
3   Wash and spin dry the lettuce, roll all the leaves into a fat cigar shape and
cut into ½ in/1 cm slices across the width of the cigar. Let the leaves unfurl
and set aside.

Assembling the sandwich:

1   Arrange the slices of avocado so they cover the bottom slice of bread.
2   Spread 1 tbsp Marie Rose sauce on top of the avocado.
3   Scatter the prawns on top.
4   Season.
5   Cover with chopped Cos leaves.
6   Top with the second slice of bread, press down gently but firmly and
slice in half.

Marie Rose Sauce

Anyone who has eaten that phenomenon known as Prawn Cocktail will have experienced the joy of Marie Rose sauce. Here's how to make it (enough for sandwiches for 2):

1 heaped tbsp mayonnaise	1 tsp Worcester Sauce
1 tbsp tomato ketchup	tiny pinch of sea salt/herb salt
freshly squeezed juice of $\frac{1}{4}$ lemon	3 or 4 grinds black pepper

Combine all the above in a small bowl and whisk vigorously with a fork for 30 seconds or so.

PRAWNS The quality (and size) of frozen prawns, usually Icelandic, available in supermarkets has risen. If you have a freezer it's definitely worthwhile buying a bag and extracting the prawns in small amounts as and when you need them. You can defrost them overnight in the fridge – place them in a bowl and cover with clingfilm. Or they will defrost at room temperature in about $\frac{1}{2}$ hour as long as they are spread out.

If you want something special, buy the beautiful tiger prawns with the bluish shells that are on most good supermarkets' fish counters. These prawns have already been frozen, so don't freeze them again at home. They will keep, as they are, in the fridge for a day or two, but are best cooked the day you buy them. Allow 3 or 4 per person for sandwiches, 5 or 6 for salads.

Pan-fry them briefly (2–3 minutes) over a high heat in a teaspoon of butter or olive oil, squeezing some fresh lemon juice over them as they cook. When they have completely changed colour and turned pink all over, remove them from the pan and place them on a plate to cool down. Alternatively you can throw them into a pan of boiling water for 2 minutes – no more or they will turn to rubber – then drain them. The shells are much easier to remove once the prawns are cooked.

★ 3   HAM AND DIJON MUSTARD   Serves 1
MAYONNAISE

We think even the best ham is improved by a little mustard. Don't buy pre-packed slimy ham, it is full of water and preservatives. Supermarkets now supply good ham roast on the bone with very few or no preservatives. Ask for it to be thinly sliced, we think lots of thin slices are better in a sandwich than one or two doorstops. Italian delis all seem to stock delicious hams, often baked with rosemary or mixed herbs and claiming to be additive-free so if you come across these do try some.

2 slices fresh bread, buttered
4–5 slices ham depending on size
   and thickness
1 tsp Dijon mustard
6 slices dill pickle (see *opposite*)
3–4 slices beef tomato

seasoning: sea salt/herb salt, freshly
   ground black pepper
small handful lettuce mix
1 tbsp mayonnaise (for mustard
   mayo see *opposite*)

Preparing the filling:

1   Wash and wipe dry the beef tomato. Remember to remove the stalk and cut out any tough white core from the stalk end. Slice the tomato across its width into slices not wider than $\frac{1}{4}$ in/$\frac{1}{2}$ cm.

2   Wash the lettuce mix and either spin dry or roll gently in a tea towel.

Assembling the sandwich:

1   Arrange the ham so it covers the bottom slice of bread.

2   Spread 1 tsp (or more) of Dijon mustard over the ham.

3   Arrange 6 slices of dill pickle.

4   Arrange 3 or 4 slices of beef tomato to cover the ham.

5   Season.

6   Cover with lettuce.

7   Spread 1 tbsp of mayonnaise on the second slice of bread and place it face down on the sandwich, press down gently but firmly and slice the way you like it.

MUSTARD MAYONNAISE   You can make a delicious mustard mayonnaise by mixing mayonnaise with Dijon mustard. For the sandwich opposite I heaped tablespoon of mayonnaise and I heaped teaspoon of mustard will give you about the right quantity. However, you may prefer to keep the mustard and mayo separate as we've suggested in the recipe. Oddly enough it does make a difference – you get the wonderful heat of the mustard setting off the ham to perfection, and the creamy mayo helping along the tomato and lettuce. It is often this sort of attention to detail which makes a sandwich extra-specially good.

DILL PICKLES   You can buy these strange, knobbly little cucumbers whole, pickled in vinegar, or ready sliced. Given the choice, buy the whole ones – they are not quite as vinegary as the sliced ones. Drain them well and slice them as thick as a £1 coin. An average pickle is about 1½ in/4 cm long and should give you 10–12 slices, probably enough for 2 sandwiches. They are brilliant with ham and pastrami, and most other cured and smoked meats, as well as cheeses such as Cheddar and Brie.

★ 4   TUNA MAYONNAISE,   Serves 1
CUCUMBER AND ROCKET

Try this on wholewheat, multigrain or rye bread. Or split a fresh Ciabatta or baguette, and remove some of the dough to make room for the filling.

2 slices fresh bread, buttered if you
   like
1 heaped tbsp tuna mayonnaise
   (see *opposite*)

small handful finely sliced
   cucumber (approx 1 oz/30 g)
seasoning: sea salt/herb salt, freshly
   ground black pepper
small handful rocket or watercress

Prepare the filling:

1   Peel about ¾ in/2 cm of cucumber and slice finely.
2   Wash the rocket or watercress in cold water, remove and discard any tough stalks and yellow or discoloured leaves, drain thoroughly and spin or pat dry.

Assembling the sandwich:

1   Spread 1 heaped tbsp tuna mayonnaise over bottom slice of bread.
2   Arrange the cucumber slices to cover the tuna.
3   Season.
4   Cover with rocket or watercress.
5   Top with the second slice of bread, press down gently but firmly and slice in half.

Best-ever Tuna Mayonnaise

Please use line-caught, dolphin-friendly tuna. For the purposes of tuna mayonnaise it is best to use tuna canned in brine rather than oil. (Tuna is an oily fish anyway, and mayonnaise obviously has a certain amount of oil. Any more oil could result in an overdose.)

5 oz/150 g tinned dolphin-friendly
  tuna in brine
1 tsp lemon zest
freshly squeezed juice ½ lemon

2 fresh firm spring onions
1 heaped tbsp mayonnaise
1 tsp Worcester sauce
seasoning: sea salt/herb salt, freshly
  ground black pepper

1   Drain the tuna and put in a clean dry bowl. Add the lemon zest and lemon juice and mix it all together with a fork.

2   Remove the outside layer from the spring onions. Chop ¼ in/½ cm from the white root end and discard. Holding the white end upwards, rinse the spring onions under a running cold tap. Shake off the water and wipe dry. Starting from the white end, slice them very finely (slices shouldn't be thicker than ⅛ in/2 mm). Keep on slicing well into the green part of the onion as long as it's firm. Add these slices to the tuna.

3   Add the mayonnaise, the Worcester sauce, a tiny pinch of sea salt or herb salt (remember that the tuna will already be salty from the brine) and 4 or 5 grinds of black pepper. Mix everything together using a fork.

★   *This makes enough for two very large sandwiches. Double or triple the quantities if you need more.*

If you need to store it, put clingfilm over the top to stop it drying out (have you ever seen brown crusts on tuna mayonnaise – yuk!) and it will keep in the fridge for a few days.

★ 5   CHICKEN BREAST, AVOCADO,   Serves 1
CHARGRILLED RED PEPPERS,
SALSA VERDE

This is a seriously filled sandwich. The Italian Pugliese bread, which is white and has just the right amount of doughiness for this combination of ingredients, is the one to go for, otherwise white cottage loaf, or Ciabatta (in which case cut a loaf in half, trim off the end and split like a pitta bread).

2 slices bread
½ perfectly ripe avocado
1 tbsp mayonnaise
½ freshly cooked chicken breast
    (see notes on page 41) or 2–3
    oz/55–85 g cold roast chicken
2–3 slices/strips (approx 2 oz/55 g)
    chargrilled and skinned red
    pepper (see opposite)

seasoning: sea salt/herb salt, freshly
    ground black pepper
small handful (½ oz/15 g) salad
    leaves (Cos/Escarole/radicchio/
    rocket, etc)
1 tbsp salsa verde (see opposite)

Preparing the filling:

1   Whether you use freshly cooked chicken breast or left-overs from a roast, shred the chicken by hand into smallish pieces.

2   Cut the avocado in half top to bottom. Peel the stoneless half, lay it face down on the chopping surface and slice into ¼ in/½ cm slices, cutting lengthways. (The remaining half can be stored in the fridge for a day or two – leave the stone in place, squeeze some fresh lemon juice over the flesh, wrap tightly in clingfilm.)

3   Whether you have prepared the peppers yourself or have bought them ready prepared, make sure that the skins have been removed – it will not spoil the taste and will improve the texture.

Assembling the sandwich:

1   Arrange the slices of avocado so they cover the bottom slice of bread.
2   Spread 1 tbsp mayonnaise on top of the avocado.
3   Arrange the shredded chicken breast over the mayo.
4   Arrange the slices/strips of pepper so they cover the chicken.
5   Season.

6   Cover with salad leaves.

7   Spread 1 tbsp salsa verde on the second slice of bread, place face down on the sandwich, press down gently but firmly and slice in half.

CHARGRILLED RED PEPPERS   Red peppers become really delicious once they've been grilled – the flesh turns silky and juicy and takes on a wonderful smoky flavour. You can buy ready-grilled red peppers at some supermarkets now (Waitrose, Tesco and Sainsbury's) and at most good Italian delis. If you want to prepare them yourself, here's how:

Choose a fairly large (no smaller than 4 in/10 cm) red pepper. Cut it into quarters, remove the stalk, pith and seeds and lay the quarters on the grill skin side up. Place under a hot grill, close to the heat, until the skins are thoroughly blackened and blistered. Sophie Grigson has a brilliant method for removing the skins: drop the grilled pepper slices into a plastic bag, knot the ends and leave until the pepper is cool enough to handle. The captured steam loosens the skins so that they are easy to remove.

If you have a griddle pan with ridges you can blacken the peppers in this using a little olive oil to grease the pan and cook over a high heat. Griddle peppers on both sides but remember to remove the skins once they are cool.

Salsa Verde

This is a combination of flat-leaf parsley, garlic, lemon juice and zest, capers, olive oil, mustard and anchovies. The anchovies are optional. Don't make this at home unless you have a food processor – good supermarkets and delis should be able to provide you with a decent version. For home-made salsa verde here goes:

½ oz/15 g flat leaf parsley leaves, thoroughly washed and dried

1 tbsp capers, rinsed in water and well drained

1 fresh firm garlic clove (not too large)

1 tsp freshly grated lemon zest

1 tsp freshly squeezed lemon juice

1 anchovy, well drained (optional)

small pinch sea salt

2 or 3 grinds black pepper

½ tsp Dijon mustard

1–2 tbsp olive oil

Put all the ingredients, except the olive oil, in the processor (preferably a mini-blender) and blend for 1 minute. Add the olive oil gradually until the salsa becomes creamy in consistency. This will give you enough salsa verde for 4 sandwiches and will keep in the fridge for up to a week in an airtight container. You can use it straight from the fridge.

★ 6   SPICY CHICKEN, YOGHURT,   Serves 1
MINT MAYO, WATERCRESS

The secret of this sandwich is that the chicken shouldn't be over-spicy, otherwise the other ingredients won't get a look in. If you can find caraway bread, or rye bread with caraway seeds, buy it for this sandwich — the combination of tastes is brilliant.

2 slices rye and caraway bread, buttered (with unsalted butter) if you like
2–3 oz/55–85 g spicy chicken (see below)
finely sliced fresh cucumber

1 tbsp yoghurt and mint mayo (see opposite)
seasoning: sea salt/herb salt, freshly ground black pepper
small handful of watercress

Preparing the filling:

1   Prepare the spicy chicken and mint mayo (see below and opposite).
2   Peel about ¾ in/2 cm of cucumber and slice as finely as possible.
3   Wash and spin dry the watercress, taking care to pinch off any thick stalks and remove any discoloured or limp leaves.

Assembling the sandwich:

1   Spread the spicy chicken over the bottom slice of bread.
2   Arrange the cucumber slices so they cover the chicken.
3   Spread 1 heaped tbsp yoghurt and mint mayo over the cucumber.
4   Season.
5   Cover with watercress.
6   Top with the second slice of bread, press down gently but firmly and slice in half.

SPICY CHICKEN   This is very much a matter of taste and there are many different spices to choose from. We suggest you go for a tikka powder or paste, adding cayenne pepper or chilli powder if you want it any hotter. Follow the instructions on the pack or jar – they will usually tell you to combine the spice with natural yoghurt and a little oil such as sunflower.

Tikka powder   Whisk 1 tbsp powder into ½ tsp sunflower oil and 1 tsp lemon juice. Add 1 tbsp mild and creamy natural yoghurt, whisk again and taste. Add a little more tikka powder or cayenne pepper/chilli powder to taste.

Tikka paste   Mix 1 tbsp paste with 1 tbsp yoghurt. Roughly shred or chop a freshly cooked chicken breast. Add the pieces of chicken to the spicy mix and stir thoroughly so the chicken is well coated. (If you do this while the chicken is still warm it will absorb the spicy flavours better.)

Yoghurt and Mint Mayo

This tastes wonderfully fresh and is essential with the spicy chicken. Here are 2 ways to make it:

1 level tbsp good-quality mint sauce (make sure you get more mint than sauce – drain off the vinegar)	1 heaped tbsp mayonnaise 1 level tbsp thick, mild and creamy natural yoghurt

Whisk these together in a small bowl using a fork.

2 tbsp fresh mint leaves, thoroughly washed and dried 1 level tbsp mayonnaise	1 level tbsp thick, mild and creamy natural yoghurt 1 tsp freshly squeezed lemon juice

Either chop the mint very very finely and whisk into the mayonnaise and yoghurt with the lemon juice *or* put all the ingredients into a mini-blender and whizz for half a minute.

7

PRET'S VEGETARIAN CLUB
WITH FRESH HERB MAYO

Serves 1

In our shops we make this sandwich on walnut bread. If you can't find walnut bread, try Cranks Organic Wholemeal with sunflower seeds, available from leading supermarkets.

Yellow and red peppers are sweet and crunchy and give the sandwich brilliant colour. Choose small peppers, no larger than 3 in/7.5 cm.

2 slices walnut or sunflower seed bread
2 heaped tbsp low-fat cream cheese or cottage cheese
½ perfectly ripe avocado
2 tbsp fresh herb mayo (see *opposite*)
1 small red pepper

1 small yellow pepper
3–4 slices beef tomato
seasoning: sea salt/herb salt, freshly ground black pepper
small handful lettuce mix (Cos, radicchio, rocket)

Preparing the filling:

1 Wash and dry the peppers (*see page 17 for notes on peppers*). Cut off the top ½ in/1 cm including the stalk, and scoop out the pith and seeds. Slice 4 fine rings from each pepper no wider than ¼ in/½ cm (you'll need a good sharp knife for this). Wrap the remaining pepper in clingfilm and store in the fridge for up to 3 days.

2 Cut the avocado in half top to bottom. Peel the stoneless half, lay it face down on the chopping surface and slice into ¼ in/½ cm slices, cutting lengthways. (The remaining half can be stored in the fridge for a day or two – leave the stone in place, squeeze some fresh lemon juice over the flesh, wrap tightly in clingfilm.)

3 Wash and wipe dry the beef tomato. Remember to remove the stalk and cut out any tough white core from the stalk end. Slice the tomato across its width into slices not wider than ¼ in/½ cm.

4 Wash the lettuce mix and spin or pat dry.

Assembling the sandwich:

1 Spread 1 heaped tbsp cream cheese over the bottom slice of bread.

2 Arrange avocado slices so that they cover the cheese.

3 Spread 1 tbsp fresh herb mayo over the avocado.

4 Arrange 4 rings red pepper and 4 rings yellow pepper so that all the pepper rings are evenly distributed over the avocado.

5 Cover with 3 or 4 slices beef tomato.

6 Season.

7 Cover with lettuce mix.

8 Top with the second slice of bread, press down gently but firmly and slice in half.

Fresh Herb Mayo

Home-made fresh herb mayo tastes really wonderful. It's quick and easy to make and well worth the effort. This recipe will make herb mayo for 2 sandwiches and enough for a delicious dip for the rest of the red and yellow peppers in the following recipe – add some carrot and celery sticks too.

2 heaped tbsp flat-leaf parsley leaves, thoroughly washed and dried

2 tbsp fresh tarragon leaves, thoroughly washed and dried

1 tbsp chopped chives

1 tsp finely grated lemon zest

freshly squeezed juice of $\frac{1}{4}$ lemon

5 tbsp mayonnaise

small pinch sea salt or herb salt

freshly ground black pepper

Put all the ingredients into a mini-blender and whizz for half a minute *or* chop all the herbs by hand – put them into a mug or jam jar and snip at them with scissors until they're finely chopped (this is surprisingly quick). Then add the lemon zest and juice, the mayonnaise, salt and pepper, and whisk everything together with a fork.

This will keep for up to a week in the fridge in a sealed container.

8

GOATS' CHEESE, PINK PEPPERCORNS, TOMATO, ROCKET

Serves 1

We make this sandwich on walnut bread. Try to find walnut bread if you can, walnut and goats' cheese is such a great combination. If you can't, use multigrain or wholemeal or whatever you prefer and scatter a tablespoon of chopped walnuts over the cheese. The French dressing makes the tomatoes taste extra good and most of it will be absorbed by the goats' cheese, preventing it from being too dry.

2 slices walnut bread
1 heaped tbsp, approx 1½ oz/45 g
    goats' cheese (see *opposite*)
1 tsp pink peppercorns, well
    drained (see *opposite*)
3–4 slices beef tomato

1 tsp French dressing (see *page 11*
    for notes on French dressing)
seasoning: sea salt/herb salt, freshly
    ground black pepper
small handful fresh rocket

Preparing the filling:

1   Wash and wipe dry the tomato. Remember to remove the stalk and cut out any tough white core from the stalk end. Slice the tomato across its width into slices not wider than ¼ in/ ½ cm.
2   Wash and dry the rocket, taking care to pick out any yellowed leaves and remove excessively stalky bits.
3   Put the drained peppercorns on a chopping board. Using the back of a wooden spoon, crush them lightly, taking care not to let them shoot off the board.

Assembling the sandwich:

1   Spread the heaped tbsp goats' cheese over the bottom slice of bread.
2   Scatter the crushed pink peppercorns on top of the cheese.
3   Arrange 3 or 4 slices of beef tomato on top.
4   Dribble 1 tsp of French dressing over the tomato slices.
5   Season.
6   Cover with rocket.
7   Top with the second slice of bread, press down gently but firmly and slice in half.

GOATS' CHEESE   We buy Innes (English) goats' cheese. This is being stocked more and more widely and you will probably find it in large supermarkets. English goats' cheeses (apart from Innes) tend to be milder than the French ones; as a rule of thumb if you buy French you will probably get a tastier cheese. If it has a rind on it, remove this before using the cheese in the sandwich.

PINK PEPPERCORNS   These are usually stored in brine. Don't buy ones which are stored in vinegar, they seem to have an unpleasant pickled taste which spoils their own bite. Brands to look out for are Porters and Taylor & Lake.

It's important to crush them lightly with the back of a wooden spoon before you use them; bite in to a whole peppercorn unexpectedly and you might find it too much.

Crushed pink peppercorns are wonderful with meat and a great addition to sauces and salad dressings when you want a bit of extra bite.

9

SMOKED SALMON, CREAM CHEESE, DILL AND MUSTARD SAUCE, WATERCRESS

This is especially good on rye or caraway bread, the darker the better.

2 slices (dark) rye bread, buttered (with unsalted butter) if you like

1 heaped tbsp low-fat cream cheese

2 oz/55 g smoked salmon (see *opposite*)

freshly ground black pepper

$\frac{1}{2}$ tbsp dill and mustard sauce (see *opposite*) available in all supermarkets

small handful ($\frac{1}{2}$ oz/15 g) watercress

Preparing the filling:

Wash and spin dry the watercress, taking care to pinch off any thick stalks and remove any discoloured or limp leaves.

Assembling the sandwich:

1   Spread 1 heaped tbsp low-fat cream cheese over the bottom slice of bread.
2   Arrange 2 oz/55 g smoked salmon so that it covers the slice.
3   Add 2 or 3 grinds black pepper.
4   Spread 1 tbsp dill and mustard sauce over the smoked salmon.
5   Cover with watercress.
6   Top with the second slice of bread, press down gently but firmly and slice in half.

SMOKED SALMON   You can buy this pre-packed and ready-sliced almost anywhere. Avoid smoked salmon that is an overly bright orange and shiny, it often means it is saltier, tougher and greasier than it ought to be. It should be moist and a creamy pink/orange. Smoked salmon freezes well: you can open a fresh pack, use what you need, wrap the rest of the pack tightly in clingfilm (or your freezer will smell forever of smoked fish) and freeze it. Remember it can be frozen only once. If you feel like a change, buy smoked salmon trout which has a more delicate flavour.

DILL AND MUSTARD SAUCE   This is the classic partner for gravlax: the delicious Scandinavian marinated salmon. We think that it tastes wonderful with smoked salmon too.

There are many good Dill and Mustard sauces available ready-made in jars. If you prefer to make your own here's how:

2 tsp muscovado or molasses sugar	2 heaped tbsp finely chopped fresh
I tsp fresh lemon juice	dill
2 tsp Dijon mustard	sea salt/herb salt and freshly
I tsp walnut oil	ground black pepper
I heaped tbsp mayonnaise	

Whisk the dark sugar and lemon juice together until the sugar has dissolved. Add the mustard, walnut oil and mayonnaise, whisking all the time. Finally add the fresh dill, season with a small pinch of sea salt or herb salt and freshly ground black pepper and whisk everything together. This sauce is meant to be fairly runny, if it seems too runny add a little more mayonnaise.

Alternatively, put all the ingredients in a mini blender and whizz for I minute.

Try to make the sauce the day before you want to use it so that the fresh dill has time to flavour the sauce fully. Store in an airtight jar in the fridge. The sauce will last for up to a week and is excellent with white fish and grilled or barbequed chicken.

This is our best-selling sandwich, and though it may not be exotic, everybody loves it. It's simple: great bacon, great chicken, fresh salad, carefully made all equals unbeatable taste.

2 slices fresh bread, buttered
2–3 oz/55–85 g freshly cooked
    chicken breast
1 heaped tbsp mayonnaise
½ tsp Dijon mustard (optional)
4–5 rashers streaky bacon

3–4 slices beef tomato
seasoning: sea salt/herb salt, freshly
    ground black pepper
small handful (½ oz/15 g) lettuce
    mix: Cos, radicchio, etc

Preparing the filling:

1   Dry-fry or grill the streaky bacon rashers until crispy (see *page 76 for notes on bacon*).

2   Shred the freshly cooked chicken breast (see *page 41 for notes on chicken*) into smallish pieces.

3   Wash and wipe dry the tomato. Remember to remove the stalk and cut out any tough white core from the stalk end. Slice the tomato across its width into slices not wider than ¼ in/½ cm.

4   Wash and spin dry the lettuce mix.

5   If you like your mayonnaise a bit mustardy, whisk the ½ teaspoon of Dijon mustard into the heaped tablespoon of mayonnaise before spreading it on the sandwiches. This is a personal thing – some like it a bit hot, some don't, you decide.

Assembling the sandwich:

1   Arrange the shredded chicken breast over the bottom slice of bread.

2   Spread the heaped tbsp mayonnaise over the chicken.

3   Arrange 4 or 5 crispy bacon rashers over the chicken and mayo.

4   Arrange 3 or 4 slices beef tomato to cover the bacon.

5   Season.

6   Cover with lettuce mix.

7   Top with the second slice of bread, press down gently but firmly and slice in half.

★ 11   PRAWNS, TOMATO AND PARSLEY   Serves 1

This tastes wonderfully fresh and light and is a low-calorie (under 300 calories) sandwich. You will need to buy thin sliced Granary® or wholemeal bread and use low-calorie mayonnaise. If you're not worried about calories then make it with your usual choice of bread and Hellman's mayonnaise.

2 slices of Granary® or wholemeal
  bread
1 tbsp low-calorie mayonnaise
2 oz/ 55 g frozen prawns
½ tsp freshly squeezed lemon juice
pinch of paprika (optional)

½ tsp freshly grated lemon zest
1 heaped tbsp flat-leaf parsley
  leaves
3–4 slices beef tomato
seasoning: sea salt/herb salt, freshly
  ground black pepper

Preparing the filling:

1   Defrost the prawns overnight in the fridge or at room temperature for 1 hour. When defrosted, squeeze the lemon juice over them, plus 1 or 2 grinds of black pepper.

2   Wash and dry the parsley leaves, put them in a mug or jam jar and cut them using scissors.

Assembling the sandwich:

1   Spread 1 tbsp low-calorie mayo over the bottom slice of bread.

2   Arrange the prawns over the mayo.

3   Sprinkle a pinch of paprika and the lemon zest over the prawns.

4   Scatter the chopped parsley over the prawns.

5   Arrange 3 or 4 slices beef tomato over the prawns.

6   Season.

7   Top with the second slice of bread, press down gently but firmly and slice in half.

SMOKED SALMON DELUXE Serves 1

As its name suggests, a really luxurious, go-for-broke smoked salmon sandwich. Best on rye or dark bread.

2 slices of rye bread, buttered with
    unsalted butter
2 oz/55 g smoked salmon, ready sliced
½ tsp creamed horseradish
freshly squeezed juice of ¼ lemon
seasoning: herb salt, freshly ground
    black pepper

4 fresh red onion rings
small handfull (½ oz/15 g)
    watercress
1 heaped tbsp egg mayonnaise
small pinch mild curry powder
    (optional)

Preparing the filling:

1   Peel the papery outside skin from the red onion. Cutting across the
onion, slice off the top ¾ in/2 cm and discard. Cut 2 very fine slices, no wider
than about ⅛ in/2 mm. Choose 4 of the largest single sings from these slices
and set these aside. (Wrap the remaining onion and sliced rings in clingflim
and store in the fridge – it will keep for several days).
2   For egg mayonnaise, see *page 76*.
3   Wash and dry the watercress, taking care to pinch out any thick stalks
and remove any discoloured or limp leaves.

Assembling the sandwich:

On 1 slice of bread:
1   Arrange the smoked salmon slices so they cover the bread.
2   Spread ½ tsp horseradish on top of the smoked salmon.
3   Squeeze ¼ lemon over the smoked salmon using a tea-strainer to catch
any pips.
4   Add 2 or 3 grinds of black pepper
5   Arrange 4 fine rings of red onion over the salmon.
6   Cover with watercress.

On the second slice:
7   Spread 1 heaped tbsp egg mayonnaise.
8   Sprinkle a small pinch herb salt and some freshly ground black pepper
and a small pinch mild curry powder if you wish.
9   Lift the egg mayo slice and place face down on top of the smoked salmon
and watercress. Press down gently but firmly and slice the way you like it.

★ 13 **POACHED SALMON AND WATERCRESS** Serves 1

Choose Granary® or rye bread.

2 slices fresh bread, buttered
2½ oz/75 g freshly poached salmon
   (see *over, page 98*)
I heaped tbsp dill mayonnaise (see
   p. 99)
I extra sprig of fresh dill

finely sliced cucumber
seasoning: sea salt/herb salt, freshly
   ground black pepper
small handful (½ oz/15 g)
   watercress

Preparing the filling:

I   Peel the outside skin from ¾ –1¼ in/2–3 cm of a cucumber, using a potato peeler if you have one, and slice the cucumber very finely. Sprinkle a pinch of sea salt over the slices and set aside.

2   Wash the dill under cold running water and shake dry. Tear the feathery leaves from the main stalk and chop roughly.

3   Wash and dry the watercress, taking care to pinch out any thick stalks and remove any discoloured or limp leaves.

Assembling the sandwich:

I   Spread the poached salmon over the bottom slice of bread taking care not to squash the flakes of salmon.

2   Carefully spread I heaped tbsp dill mayo over the salmon.

3   Sprinkle the fresh chopped dill over the mayo.

4   Arrange the finely sliced cucumber to cover the salmon and dill mayo.

5   Add 2 or 3 grinds of black pepper.

6   Cover with watercress.

7   Top with the second slice of bread, press down gently but firmly and slice in half.

Poaching Fresh Salmon

This is dead easy and takes no time at all. There are two ways to do it: in a saucepan on the hob, or in an ovenproof dish in the oven. For poached salmon for sandwiches for 2 you will need:

6 oz/170 g salmon fillet
enough kitchen foil to wrap around
   the salmon
1 tsp Marigold Bouillon powder *or*
   fish seasoning

or

1 sprig of dill/thyme/rosemary
freshly ground black pepper
1 tsp salted butter

Put the salmon fillet, skin side down, in the middle of the kitchen foil. Sprinkle the teaspoon of bouillon powder and a couple of grinds of black pepper on top of the salmon and dot the butter over the top. If you want to use fresh herbs, leave out the bouillon powder and put the sprig of fresh dill/thyme/rosemary over the butter. Wrap the kitchen foil up over the salmon and turn the ends over so that it is watertight. Put the salmon package either:

1   in a saucepan and pour a little water into the bottom of the saucepan so that it comes about ½ in/1 cm up the side of the package. Cover the saucepan and place on a medium heat for 15 mins so that the salmon cooks in the steam of the boiling water. You may need to check the pan every so often to make sure it doesn't boil dry – add more water as needed.

or

2   in a heatproof dish. Pour water around the salmon in the same way as above, cover if possible (not essential), and put into a preheated oven (375°F/190°C/Gas Mark 5) for 20 minutes.

In both cases let the salmon cool down in its package before unwrapping it, as this will prevent it from drying out.

Dill Mayonnaise

Well worth making at home.

2 heaped tbsp dill leaves,
   thoroughly washed and dried
4 heaped tbsp mayonnaise

pinch herb salt
freshly ground black pepper

Chop the dill finely in a mug or jam jar using scissors. Add the mayonnaise and seasoning and whisk with a fork.

You can make this even more special by adding 2 teaspoons walnut oil and 1 teaspoon fresh lemon juice. This will keep in the fridge for up to a week and will give you plenty for 4 rounds of sandwiches. Or just serve it with poached salmon cooled down to room temperature and a simple green salad.

PRET'S ALL-DAY BREAKFAST Serves 1

We think that Cumberland sausages are about the best for this sandwich. They seem to have just the right amount of spice. You don't want anything too fancy or it won't mix happily with eggs and bacon; if you can't find Cumberland, use your favourite breakfast sausage.

2 slices fresh bread, buttered
1 heaped tbsp egg mayonnaise
1 freshly cooked average-size
   Cumberland sausage (not
   chipolata)
1 tbsp tomato ketchup

4–5 rashers streaky bacon
3–4 slices beef tomato
1 tbsp mayonnaise
seasoning: sea salt/herb salt, freshly
   ground black pepper
½ punnet of baby (mustard) cress

Preparing the filling:

1   Slice the cooked sausage lengthways into 3 or 4 strips.

2   Dry fry or grill the streaky bacon until crispy (see *page 76 for notes on bacon*).

3   For egg mayonnaise, see *page 76*.

4   Wash and wipe dry the tomato. Remember to remove its stalk and cut out the tough white core from the stalk end. Slice the tomato across its width into slices not wider than ¼ in/½ cm.

5   Cut the baby cress from its box using scissors or a sharp knife. Rinse it in a sieve under cold running water and shake well to drain.

Assembling the sandwich:

1   Spread 1 heaped tbsp egg mayonnaise over the bottom slice of bread.

2   Arrange 3 or 4 slices of Cumberland sausage over the egg mayo.

3   Squirt a large 'O' of tomato ketchup if you have a plastic squeezy bottle; if you have a glass bottle, 1 tbsp spread over the sausage should be about right.

4   Arrange 4 or 5 rashers of crispy bacon over the sausage.

5   Arrange 3 or 4 slices beef tomato to cover the bacon.

6   Spread 1 tbsp mayo over the tomato.

7   Season.

8   Scatter the baby cress over the tomato and mayo.

9   Top with the second slice of bread, press down gently but firmly and slice in half.

★ 15   **MATURE CHEDDAR WITH**   Serves 1
                   FRUIT CHUTNEY

For cheese lovers. Buy the best cheddar you can afford – mature cheddar is worth the extra cost. Choose a fairly strong flavoured chutney – plum, onion, apple, green tomato, etc, to complement the cheese.

2 slices fresh buttered bread
2–3 oz/55–85 g mature Cheddar
   cheese
1 heaped tbsp fruit chutney
3–4 slices beef tomato
1 tbsp mayonnaise

seasoning: sea salt/herb salt, freshly
   ground black pepper
small handful ($\frac{1}{2}$ oz/15 g)
   watercress or lettuce mix –
   Cos, Escarole, radicchio

Preparing the filling:

1   Slice the cheese into very thin slices.
2   Wash and wipe dry the tomato. Remember to remove the stalk and cut out any tough white core from the stalk end. Slice the tomato across its width into slices not wider than $\frac{1}{4}$ in/$\frac{1}{2}$ cm.
3   Wash and spin dry the watercress or lettuce mix, taking care to pinch out any thick stalks and remove any discoloured or limp leaves.

Assembling the sandwich:

1   Cover the bottom slice of bread with cheese.
2   Spread 1 heaped tbsp fruit chutney over the cheese.
3   Cover with 3 or 4 slices of tomato.
4   Spread 1 tbsp mayo over the tomato.
5   Season.
6   Cover with watercress lettuce mix.
7   Top with the second slice of bread, press down gently but firmly and slice in half.

★   *For more cheese sandwiches, see no.s 8, 24, 25, 30, 32.*

PASTRAMI AND DILL PICKLE ON RYE

Serves 1

This is an American classic, it has a hundred variations and is sold in practically every deli in the US. Pastrami is beef brisket which has been cured with herbs, ginger and peppercorns and smoked.* You can buy pastrami from most supermarket deli counters. It is traditionally served on warm rye bread. It also tastes good on sourdough bread, walnut bread, or any other nut bread.

2 slices of rye bread, buttered
   (with unsalted butter) if you like
1 tbsp sour cream or crème
   fraîche
1 tbsp cream cheese
1 tsp balsamic vinegar
2 oz/55 g best pastrami, ready sliced

6 slices dill pickle (see *page 81*)
3–4 slices beef tomato
seasoning: sea salt/herb salt, freshly
   ground black pepper
½ punnet of baby (mustard) cress

Preparing the filling:

1   Slice the dill pickle (if it's not ready sliced) into slices approx. the thickness of a £1 coin.

2   Wash and wipe dry the beef tomato. Remember to remove the stalk and cut out the tough white core from the stalk end. Slice the tomato across its width into slices not wider than ¼ in/½ cm.

3   In a small bowl combine the cream cheese and the sour cream, using a whisk if you have one – a fork is fine, but whisk briskly. The mix should look whipped. Add the teaspoon of balsamic vinegar and whisk in.

4   Cut the baby cress from its box using scissors or a sharp knife. Rinse it in a sieve under cold running water and shake it well to drain it.

5   If you want to warm the pastrami, wrap it in kitchen foil and heat it in the microwave for 30 secs or a hot oven for 3–4 mins.

* Our pastrami is made from South American grass-fed beef.

Assembling the sandwich:

1 Spread the sour cream/cheese mix over the bottom slice of bread.
2 Lay the pastrami slices so that they cover the cream cheese.
3 Arrange 6 slices of dill pickle on top.
4 Arrange 3 to 4 slices of beef tomato to cover the pastrami and dill pickle.
5 Season.
6 Scatter the baby cress over the tomato.
7 Top with the second slice of bread, press down gently but firmly and slice in half.

★ *If the pastrami is warm, eat the sandwich immediately.*

★ 17　SMOKED SALMON TARTARE, Serves 1
SPRING ONIONS, CAPERS,
TARRAGON AND SOUR CREAM

You can use either smoked salmon, or gravlax, or smoked salmon trout. Of the three, we think smoked salmon works best – it has the strongest flavour and stands up well to all other ingredients. Some smoked salmons are oilier than others, try to avoid the greasy ones.

Try this as a sandwich on rye bread with caraway, failing that black rye, or granary. Even though there is a fair amount of sour cream, spreading both bits of bread with some unsalted butter will make this sandwich a truly luxurious experience.

**2 slices rye bread, spread with
  unsalted butter**
**1 tbsp tarragon leaves, thoroughly
  washed and dried**
1 tbsp sour cream
1 tbsp mayonnaise

for the tartare:
2 oz/55 g smoked salmon
1 tbsp capers, drained and rinsed
freshly squeezed juice of $\frac{1}{4}$ lemon
1 tsp freshly grated lemon zest
2 crushed black peppercorns
1 tsp walnut oil
1 spring onion

Preparing the filling:

1　Chop the smoked salmon and the capers roughly, put in a bowl with the lemon juice and zest, 2 crushed black peppercorns, 1 tsp walnut oil and leave for at least half an hour.

2　Trim the spring onion, remove the outer skin, then run it under a tap with the green end pointing down to sluice out any grit. Chop it very finely, and use some of the green as well as the white.

3　Add the chopped spring onion to the salmon tartare just before you want to make the sandwich, otherwise the spring onion will overpower everything.

4　Chop the tarragon leaves, very briefly, in a mug or jam jar using scissors. It doesn't matter if some of the leaves don't even get chopped in half. Add the sour cream and mayonnaise and stir together.

Assembling the sandwich:

1   Spread the salmon tartare over one slice of buttered bread.

2   Spread the sour cream and tarragon mayo over the other slice, and place face down on the salmon.

3   Press down gently but firmly and slice in half.

★   *To tell you the truth this wonderful smoked salmon tartare is best of all eaten on some hot fresh toast, spread with the sour cream and tarragon mix (which will melt slightly) and topped with the smoked salmon tartare. You could serve this as a starter or light supper accompanied by a rocket salad dressed with fresh lemon juice, walnut oil and sea salt.*

HAM, CREAM CHEESE, TOMATO, MUSTARD, LETTUCE

Serves 1

This is particularly delicious in a freshly baked baguette, or Ciabatta. You can buy oven-ready baguettes, or most supermarkets sell pretty decent versions of baguettes freshly baked on the premises. Look out for baguettes which are described as 'authentic French' or 'made with French flour'. Allow about 8–10 in/20–25 cm of baguette per person.

8–10 in/20–25 cm fresh baguette
    or $\frac{1}{3}$ Ciabatta loaf, buttered if
    you like
2 heaped tbsp low-fat cream cheese
2–3 oz/55–85 g thinly sliced ham
2 tsp Dijon mustard

1 medium-sized tomato
1 heaped tbsp mayonnaise
seasoning: sea salt/herb salt, freshly
    ground black pepper
1 handful lettuce mix – Cos,
    Escarole, radicchio

Preparing the filling:

1 Wash and wipe dry the tomato. Remember to remove the stalk and cut out any tough white core from the stalk end. Slice the tomato across its width into slices not wider than $\frac{1}{4}$ in/$\frac{1}{2}$ cm.

2 Wash and spin dry the lettuce mix and remove any large or thick stalks and any discoloured or limp leaves.

Assembling the baguette:

1 Split the baguette down the centre but keep it joined at the outer edge. You may need to remove some dough from inside the top half or you won't fit everything in.

2 Spread 2 heaped tbsp cream cheese over the bottom half.

3 Layer on the slices of ham, folding it as necessary so it fits the baguette.

4 Spread about 2 tsp Dijon mustard over the ham, or to taste.

5 Arrange the tomato slices to cover the ham.

6 Spread 1 tbsp mayonnaise over the tomato slices and season.

7 Arrange the lettuce (you may have to tear it into smaller pieces) on top of the tomato.

8 Clamp the top of the baguette over firmly. If you're not going to eat it straight away wrap it tightly in greaseproof paper to stop the filling from escaping.

★ 19 **SMOKED TROUT OR MACKEREL,** Serves 1
HORSERADISH MAYO, WATERCRESS

This is a strong sandwich, bursting with flavour. Try to find rye bread with caraway, otherwise wholegrain will be fine.

2 slices fresh bread, spread with
   unsalted butter
2–3 oz/55–85 g smoked trout or
   smoked undyed mackerel
¼ lemon

1 heaped tbsp mayonnaise
1 tsp horseradish sauce
seasoning: sea salt/herb salt, freshly
   ground black pepper
small handful watercress

Preparing the filling:

1   Remove the skin and any bones from the smoked trout or mackerel. Squeeze lemon juice over it.

2   Mix together the mayonnaise and the horseradish.

3   Wash and spin dry the watercress, taking care to pinch out any thick stalks and remove any discoloured or limp leaves.

Assembling the sandwich:

1   Spread the smoked fish over the bottom slice of bread, handle it gently and don't mash it.

2   Spread 1 heaped tbsp of horseradish mayo over the smoked fish.

3   Add 2 or 3 grinds black pepper.

4   Sprinkle sea salt/herb salt – this may not be necessary, smoked fish is fairly salty.

5   Cover with watercress.

6   Top with the second slice of bread, press down gently but firmly and slice in half.

★ 20   **CRUNCHY PEANUT BUTTER,**   Serves 1
REDCURRANT JELLY, BANANA

Peanut butter and jelly – not everybody's idea of a great sandwich, but for those who love it here's an especially delicious version. We particularly like Whole Earth's crunchy peanut butter, they have an organic version which we strongly recommend. Otherwise good old Sunpat does the trick.

Look out for speciality seed (fruit) and nut breads. If you want to go all the way, spread some unsalted butter on both slices of bread.

2 slices fresh bread, spread with
   unsalted butter
1 heaped tbsp crunchy peanut
   butter

1 heaped tbsp redcurrant jelly
   (Tiptree)
1 tsp freshly grated orange zest
1 small perfectly ripe banana

Preparing the filling:

1   Peel and slice the banana, removing any long strings of pith and cutting away any very brown soggy patches.

2   Wash the orange and dry it thoroughly. Take care when grating the orange not to grate into the white pith, just skim the zest from the peel

Assembling the sandwich:

1   Spread 1 heaped tbsp crunchy peanut butter over the bottom slice of bread.

2   Spread 1 heaped tbsp redcurrant jelly over the peanut butter.

3   Sprinkle 1 tsp freshly grated orange zest over the jelly.

4   Arrange the slices of banana to cover the sandwich.

5   Top with the second slice of bread, press down gently but firmly and slice in half.

21

ROAST TURKEY, CRANBERRY SAUCE, PINENUTS, WATERCRESS

Serves 1

The obvious time for this one is after Christmas or Easter when there is plenty of turkey about. If you have any turkey stuffing, substitute some slices of stuffing for some of the turkey. You can buy ready-cooked turkey from most supermarkets and delicatessens – check how long ago it was cooked.

If you haven't got any homemade cranberry sauce, leading supermarkets and good delis stock cranberry sauce in jars – the higher the fruit content, the better it will be. Try this on rye bread.

2 slices fresh bread, buttered if you like

2 oz/55 g turkey breast or leg, sliced thin, including some stuffing (optional)

1 heaped tbsp cranberry sauce

1 tbsp toasted pinenuts

1 medium-sized tomato

1 tbsp mayonnaise

seasoning: sea salt/herb salt, freshly ground pepper

small handful watercress

Preparing the filling:

1 Toast the pinenuts either under the grill or dry fry them in a non-stick pan until they turn a deep golden brown. It's really worth doing this – it makes a tremendous difference to their flavour.

2 Wash and wipe dry the tomato. Remember to remove the stalk and cut out any tough white core from the stalk end. Slice the tomato across its width into slices not wider than $\frac{1}{4}$ in/$\frac{1}{2}$ cm.

3 Wash and spin dry the watercress, taking care to pinch out any thick stalks and remove any discoloured or limp leaves.

Assembling the sandwich:

1 Arrange 2 oz/55 g of turkey meat (and stuffing) over the bottom slice of bread.

2 Spread 1 heaped tbsp cranberry sauce over the turkey.

3 Scatter 1 tbsp toasted pinenuts over the turkey and cranberry sauce.

4 Cover with slices of tomato.

5 Spread 1 tbsp mayonnaise over the tomato.

6 Season.

7 Cover with watercress.

8 Top with the second slice of bread, press down gently but firmly and slice in half.

★ 22 AVOCADO, MOZZARELLA, TOMATO, ROAST FENNEL, PINENUTS, FRESH BASIL

Serves 1

This is a seriously filled gourmet sandwich and worth every moment of effort. You could substitute salsa verde for the fresh basil; the roast fennel is optional but a great addition. If you're going on a picnic, make this sandwich (triple the quantities) in a whole loaf of Ciabatta and simply slice off sandwiches when you're ready to eat. This tastes wonderful on walnut bread, sunflower seed bread, or multigrain bread. You choose.

2 slices of bread, buttered if you like
½ perfectly ripe avocado
1 small plum tomato
seasoning: sea salt/herb salt, freshly ground pepper
6–8 leaves of fresh basil *and/or* 1 tbsp salsa verde (see *page 85*)

½ ball of mozzarella cheese (if you can't find mozzarella, ricotta, cream cheese, or even cottage cheese will work almost as well)
1 tbsp toasted pinenuts
½ fennel bulb, sliced and roasted (see *opposite*)

Preparing the filling:

1 If you want to use fennel but haven't time to roast it, clean and trim it by slicing off the stalk and leaves, removing the outside layer of flesh and slice it very finely from top to bottom, cutting away the tough core at the base. You will need 3 to 4 slices per person.

2 Cut the avocado in half top to bottom. Peel the stoneless half, lay it face down on the chopping surface and slice into ¼ in/½ cm slices, cutting lengthways. (The remaining half can be stored in the fridge for a day or two – leave the stone in place, squeeze some fresh lemon juice over the flesh, wrap tightly in clingfilm.)

3 Drain and slice the mozzarella (a serrated knife works best) not wider than ¼ in/½ cm.

4 Wash and wipe dry the plum tomato, remove the stalk and slice not wider than ¼ in/½ cm.

5 Toast the pinenuts either under the grill or dry fry them in a non-stick saucepan until they turn a deep golden brown. It's really worth doing this – it makes a tremendous difference to their flavour.

6 Wash and dry the basil leaves.

Assembling the sandwich:

1   Arrange the avocado slices so they cover the bottom slice of bread.
2   Cover with slices of plum tomato.
3   Season.
4   Arrange the fresh basil leaves over the tomato slices.
5   Cover with mozzarella slices.
6   Sprinkle 1 tbsp of toasted pinenuts over the mozzarella.
7   Arrange slices of roast (or raw) fennel to cover everything.
8   If you are using salsa verde (instead of or as well as the fresh basil) spread 1 tbsp on the top slice of bread and place it face down on top of the sandwich or top with the second slice of bread, press down gently but firmly and slice in the way you like it.

ROAST FENNEL   Raw and cooked fennel have quite different qualities. Raw fennel is crisp and juicy with a liquoricy flavour; roasted fennel becomes sweeter and creamier in texture and is particularly good with mild cheese such as mozzarella. A few of the leading supermarkets are now stocking ready grilled and roasted vegetables, including fennel, and they are worth trying. Allow about 2 oz/55 g per person for a sandwich, perhaps double that amount for a salad.

Cut the trimmed bulb lengthways into slices approx $\frac{1}{4}$ in/$\frac{1}{2}$ cm wide. Place in a shallow baking dish and sloosh olive oil, or spread butter if you prefer, over the slices. Squeeze $\frac{1}{4}$ lemon over the fennel (use a tea-strainer to catch the pips). Sprinkle a pinch of sea salt and a few grinds of black pepper over the fennel slices and put the dish in a medium oven (350°F/180°C/Gas Mark 4) for 30 minutes. The fennel should be golden brown with slight crisping at the edges. Let the fennel cool down in the dish.

★ 23   LAMB, REDCURRANT JELLY,   Serves 1
CHARGRILLED AUBERGINE

Have you got any left-over roast lamb? If you have please make this sandwich, it is stunningly good.

You can buy chargrilled aubergines from the deli counter at some of the leading supermarkets. If you can't find them or want to grill your own, see below.

2 slices of fresh bread, spread with
　unsalted butter
2–3 oz/55–85 g sliced cold roast
　lamb
1 heaped tbsp redcurrant jelly
4 slices chargrilled aubergine

seasoning: sea salt/herb salt, freshly
　ground black pepper
1 tbsp mayonnaise
$\frac{1}{2}$ punnet baby (mustard) cress
　trimmed, rinsed and drained

Grilling the aubergine:

1　Wash and wipe dry an aubergine. Cut off both ends, and slice the aubergine across its width into rounds not thicker than $\frac{1}{2}$ in/1 cm. Put these on to your clean (otherwise on kitchen foil) grillpan and either brush them with olive oil or melted butter. Sprinkle them with sea salt, a few grinds of black pepper and scatter some fresh herbs (i.e. thyme or rosemary) over them. Put them about 4 in/10 cm under a preheated medium (350°F/180°C) grill for 6–7 minutes until they start to turn a deep golden brown. Take them out, repeat the oil/butter, seasoning and herb procedure and put them back under the grill for another 5 or 6 minutes. Let them cool down in the grill pan.

2　If you have a chargrill, prepare the aubergines in the same way and chargrill them for 4 or 5 minutes on each side.

3　If you want to roast them, prepare them in the same way (one side only) and roast them in a shallow baking dish in a preheated oven (350°F/180°C) for about 30 minutes.

Assembling the sandwich:

1 Arrange the lamb slices so they cover the bottom slice of bread.

2 Spread 1 tbsp redcurrant jelly over the lamb.

3 Lay 4 or so slices of chargrilled aubergine to cover the lamb.

4 Season – unnecessary if the aubergine is already well seasoned.

5 Spread the mayonnaise over the aubergine (you can substitute a tablespoon of salsa verde (see *page 85*) instead of the mayonnaise.)

6 Scatter the baby cress over the mayo.

7 Top with the second slice of bread, press down gently but firmly and slice in half.

★ *Use your left-over grilled aubergine to make the sandwich on the following page.*

24

RICOTTA, CHARGRILLED
AUBERGINE, TOMATO, WALNUT

Serves 1

The creamy cheese and the smoky taste of the grilled aubergines is a great combination. If you want to give this sandwich a different twist substitute slow-roast tomatoes for the aubergine and fresh tomato in this recipe. See *opposite for the tomato recipe.*

2 slices fresh bread: multigrain, wholemeal, walnut or sunflower seed
1 heaped tbsp ricotta cheese
4 slices chargrilled aubergine (see page 112)

1 tbsp shelled walnuts
1 small plum tomato
seasoning: sea salt/herb salt, freshly ground black pepper
1 tbsp mayonnaise

Preparing the filling:

1 Wash and wipe dry the tomato. Remove the stalk and slice not wider than ¼ in/½ cm.
2 Pick out any dried membrane from the walnut halves, and chop roughly.

Assembling the sandwich:

1 Spread 1 heaped tbsp ricotta cheese over the bottom slice of bread.
2 Cover with 4 or so slices of chargrilled aubergine.
3 Scatter 1 tbsp chopped walnuts.
4 Cover with slices of plum tomato.
5 Season.
6 Spread 1 tbsp mayonnaise on the top slice of bread, place face down on top of the sandwich, press down gently but firmly in half.

SLOW ROAST TOMATOES   Cut 3 or 4 (more if you want) plum tomatoes in half lengthways. Put them in a shallow baking dish cut side up. Dribble a little olive oil over each tomato half, sprinkle each one with $\frac{1}{4}$ teaspoon caster sugar, a little sea salt, a few grinds of black pepper and some fresh herbs (thyme, sage, rosemary). Put them in a preheated oven 300°F/150°C/Gas mark 2 for one hour. Turn the oven down to 120°C and cook the tomatoes for a further $1\frac{1}{2}$–2 hours. They should look like sun-dried tomatoes, but they should still be fairly juicy. Let them cool down in the tray and use them in sandwiches and salads. They are especially good combined with creamy cheeses (as above) and stronger cheeses such as feta or goat.

FETA, RED ONION, YOGHURT AND MINT DRESSING

This sandwich definitely needs to be on doughy white bread. Try Pugliese, white cottage loaf or Ciabatta; but remember, if you're using Ciabatta, don't slice it, split it like you would a pitta bread – white pitta bread would also be excellent.

2 slices fresh bread, buttered if you like

2–3 oz/55–85 g feta cheese, thinly sliced

1 heaped tbsp yoghurt and mint mayo (see notes on page 87)

4 circles of red onion

3–4 slow-roast tomato halves (see page 115)

seasoning: sea salt/herb salt, freshly ground black pepper

1 tbsp black olives

small handful lettuce mix (Cos, radicchio)

Preparing the filling:

1   Peel the papery outside skin from the red onion. Cutting across the onion, slice off the top ¾ in/2 cm and discard. Cut 2 slices, not wider than about ⅛ in/2 mm. Take the 4 largest circles and set them aside. (Wrap the rest of the onion in clingfilm and store it in the fridge, it will keep for several days.)

2   Wash and spin dry the lettuce mix, taking care to remove any over-large stalks and any discoloured or limp leaves.

3   Remove the stones from the black olives (see page 15 for notes on olives). Chop them roughly.

Assembling the sandwich:

1   Arrange the sliced feta cheese so that it covers the bottom slice of bread.

2   Spread 1 heaped tbsp yoghurt and mint mayo over the feta.

3   Arrange 4 circles of red onion.

4   Arrange the slow-roast tomato halves over the onion and mayo.

5   Season.

6   Scatter 1 tbsp chopped black olives.

7   Cover with lettuce.

8   Top with the second slice of bread, press down gently but firmly and slice in half.

★ 26   CHICKEN AND TARRAGON,   Serves 1
WITH TOMATO AND SALAD

This is one of our top-selling sandwiches. We serve it on our own handmade Mediterranean bread with sun-dried tomatoes. If you can find similar speciality bread, use it. Walnut bread also works well, as does sunflower seed, multigrain, white sourdough, Pugliese, etc.

2 slices special bread, buttered if
   you like
½ freshly cooked chicken breast
   (see notes on page 41)
1 tbsp fresh tarragon leaves
1 heaped tbsp mayonnaise
1 tsp walnut oil (optional)

lemon juice (optional)
1 tomato
seasoning: sea salt/herb salt, freshly
   ground black pepper
small handful of lettuce mix –
   Escarole, Cos, radicchio

Preparing the filling:

1   Shred the chicken breast or chop roughly.

2   Wash and dry the tarragon leaves. Put them into a mug or jam jar and chop using a pair of scissors. Add the mayonnaise and stir thoroughly. (If you have time add a teaspoon of walnut oil and a quick squeeze of fresh lemon juice – delicious but not essential.)

3   Wash and wipe dry the tomato. Remember to remove the stalk and cut out any tough white core from the stalk end. Cut the tomato across into slices not wider than ¼ in/½ cm.

4   Wash and spin dry the lettuce mix, taking care to remove any large stalks and any discoloured or limp leaves.

Assembling the sandwich:

1   Arrange the shredded/chopped chicken breast so it covers the bottom slice of bread.

2   Spread 1 heaped tbsp tarragon mayo over the chicken.

3   Cover with slices of tomato.

4   Season.

5   Cover with lettuce.

6   Top with the second slice of bread, press down gently but firmly and slice in half.

SMOKED MACKEREL, FRESH DILL CUCUMBER, TOMATO

Serves 1

Beautifully made fresh dill cucumber is the secret of this sandwich. If you make quite a lot it will keep in the fridge for a couple of days and is also delicious with smoked salmon (see *page 120*).

Try to buy undyed smoked mackerel.

2 slices fresh bread, spread with
   unsalted butter
½ smoked undyed mackerel fillet
fresh dill cucumber (prepare at
   least a few hours in advance)
   (see *opposite*)

1 tomato
seasoning: freshly ground black
   pepper
1 tbsp mayonnaise

Preparing the filling:

1   Remove the skin and any bones from the mackerel fillet. Using a fork, shred the flesh so it will be easy to spread over bread. If it seems at all dry squeeze some fresh lemon juice to moisten it.

2   Wash and wipe dry the tomato. Remember to remove the stalk and cut out any tough white core from the stalk end. Slice the tomato across its width into slices no wider than ¼ in/½ cm.

Assembling the sandwich:

1   Spread the smoked mackerel over the bottom slice of bread.

2   Arrange a generous amount (2 heaped tbsp) of fresh dill cucumber over the mackerel.

3   Cover with slices of tomato.

4   Season.

5   Spread 1 tbsp mayonnaise on the top slice of bread, place face down on the sandwich, press down gently but firmly and slice in half.

Fresh Dill Cucumber

1 fresh cucumber, topped and
    tailed and peeled (with a potato
    peeler)
large pinch sea salt

4 heaped tbsp fresh dill leaves,
    thoroughly washed and dried
1 tbsp walnut oil

Slice the peeled cucumber as finely as you can. If you have a food processor, slice it through on the finest setting. The slices should be almost transparent. Put them in a bowl with a large pinch of sea salt, mix thoroughly and let them stand, covered, for a couple of hours.

You will see that some liquid has collected in the bottom of the bowl. Strain it off. Chop the fresh dill finely, add to the strained cucumber along with the tablespoon of walnut oil.

Toss the cucumber so that it is well coated with dill and oil. It's now ready to eat.

This is delicious served alongside most sandwiches or cold meat or fish.

SMOKED SALMON AND FRESH DILL CUCUMBER

Serves 1

Simple as can be and truly wonderful. Try to find smoked salmon which is unsalted – it does exist. This is a delicate sandwich: the saltier the smoked salmon, the more it will dominate the fresh dill cucumber. Or try gravlax which is marinated as opposed to smoked.

It is important that this is on white bread. If you can find brioche bread, buy it. Otherwise buy the finest white loaf you can find and slice the bread thin.

Let the butter warm to room temperature before you use it, otherwise you'll tear the bread.

2 slices fine white bread, buttered with unsalted butter
2 oz/55 g smoked salmon
¼ fresh lemon

seasoning: sea salt/herb salt, freshly ground black pepper
2 tbsp fresh dill cucumber (see page 119)

Assembling the sandwich:

1   Arrange 2 oz/55 g smoked salmon slices to cover the bottom slice of bread.
2   Squeeze the juice of the lemon quarter (through a tea-strainer to catch the pips) over the salmon.
3   Add 2 or 3 grinds of black pepper.
4   Arrange the fresh dill cucumber over the salmon.
5   Top with the second slice of bread, press down gently but firmly and slice in half.

BACON AND AVOCADO

Serves 1

This doesn't need much introduction – it's simple and very good.

2 slices fresh bread, buttered if you
    like
1 perfectly ripe avocado
4–5 rashers streaky bacon, rinds
    removed and cooked until crisp
3–4 slices beef tomato

seasoning: sea salt/herb salt, freshly
    ground black pepper
small handful (approx ½ oz/15 g)
    mixed lettuce
2 tbsp mayonnaise

Preparing the filling:

1   Dry fry or grill the bacon until crispy (see notes on page 76).
2   Cut the avocado in half top to bottom. Peel the stoneless half, lay it face
down on the chopping surface and slice into ¼ in/½ cm slices, cutting
lengthways. (The remaining half can be stored in the fridge for a day or two –
leave the stone in place, squeeze some fresh lemon juice over the flesh, wrap
tightly in clingfilm.)
3   Wash and wipe dry the tomato. Remember to remove the stalk and cut
out any tough white core from the stalk end. Slice the tomato across its width
into slices not wider than ¼ in/½ cm.
4   Wash the lettuce and spin or pat dry.

Assembling the sandwich:

1   Arrange the avocado slices so that they cover the bottom slice of bread.
2   Arrange 4 or 5 crispy bacon rashers on top of the avocado.
3   Arrange 3 or 4 slices of beef tomato to cover the bacon.
4   Season.
5   Cover with lettuce mix.
6   Spread 1 tbsp mayonnaise on the top slice of bread, place face down on
the sandwich, press down gently but firmly and slice in half.

★   To make the famous BLT, assemble the sandwich in exactly the same way
but leave out the avocado.

STILTON, CRISPY BACON, RED GRAPES, WALNUTS, FROMAGE FRAIS

Serves 1

If you are vegetarian and like blue cheese, leave out the bacon. If you can't get Stilton, try using Gorgonzola or dolcelatte. If you like Roquefort, we suggest mixing it half and half with some cream cheese or the Roquefort will overpower everything else. Try this sandwich on walnut or sourdough bread.

2 slices walnut or sourdough bread
2 oz/55 g Stilton or similar cheese
1 tbsp shelled walnuts
6–8 red grapes – try the Red
  Flame variety, they are seedless

4–5 rashers of crispy bacon
1 heaped tbsp fromage frais*
seasoning: freshly ground black
  pepper

Fromage frais is extremely light and low in calories (especially if you buy the less than 1 per cent fat variety). We think it is important to make this sandwich juicy, Stilton can be rich and dry, and the lightness of the fromage frais balances it well.

Preparing the filling:

1   Stilton is difficult to slice, especially if it is a small round or in a pot. So scoop it or cut it off the round and crumble it gently.

2   Dry fry or grill the streaky bacon until really crispy (see notes on page 76). Drain it on some crumpled kitchen paper.

3   Wash the red grapes and slice them in half top to bottom, removing any pips.

4   Remove any dried membrane from the walnut halves and chop roughly.

Assembling the sandwich:

1   Spread the Stilton gently over the bottom slice of bread.
2   Scatter 1 tbsp chopped walnuts over the Stilton.
3   Arrange the grape halves to cover the Stilton and walnuts.
4   Arrange 4–5 rashers of crispy bacon over the Stilton.
5   Spread 1 heaped tbsp fromage frais on the second slice of bread, season with some freshly ground black pepper, place it face down on top of the sandwich, press down gently but firmly and slice in half.

★   *You can try slices of perfectly ripe pear instead of the grapes and smoked turkey or ham instead of the bacon.*

31

CHICKEN, ORANGE, BLACK OLIVES OR TAPENADE WITH ROCKET

This a wonderfully fresh-tasting and surprisingly light sandwich. There is no mayonnaise, but if you need something along those lines, spread a heaped tablespoon of fromage frais under the chicken, or use unsalted butter.

2 slices fresh bread
1 heaped tbsp fromage frais
½ freshly cooked chicken breast
  (see notes on page 41)
seasoning: sea salt/herb salt, freshly
  ground black pepper

½ fresh orange – try to find Navel
  or Valencia oranges
1 tbsp stoned black olives (see page
  15) or tapenade (see opposite)
small handful fresh rocket or
  watercress

Preparing the filling:

1   Tear and slice the chicken breast into smallish pieces or chop roughly.
2   Peel the orange, divide into segments, and remove any pips and as much pith as possible. If you want to be really thoughtful, remove the skin from each of the segments. You will need 4 or 5 segments per sandwich.
3   De-stone the black olives by tearing them in half. If they are fairly soft leave them in halves. If not, chop them roughly.
4   Wash and spin dry the rocket or watercress, taking care to pinch off any thick stalks and remove any discoloured or limp leaves.

Assembling the sandwich:

1   Spread the bottom slice of bread with fromage frais or butter.
2   Arrange the chicken pieces on top.
3   Season.
4   Arrange 4 or 5 segments of orange over the chicken.
5   Scatter 1 tbsp chopped black olives over the orange. If you use tapenade instead of chopped olives, spread it on the top slice of bread and place it face down on top of the rocket or watercress.
6   Cover with rocket or watercress.
7   Top with the second slice of bread, press down gently but firmly and slice in half.

Tapenade

You can buy this ready-made olive paste in tubes, but if you want to make it at home it's easy provided you've got a blender.

Put 8 oz/225 g stoned black olives in a blender with the freshly squeezed juice of ¼ lemon, 1 small clove peeled and chopped garlic, 1 tbsp olive oil, and 1 anchovy fillet. Whizz until everything is thoroughly blended. If you keep the tapenade in an airtight jar in the fridge it will last for several weeks.

It's delicious spread thickly on hot toast and topped with a few slices of tomato.

RICOTTA OR COTTAGE CHEESE, PESTO, TOMATO AND ROCKET Serves 1

We suggest ricotta or cottage cheese but any mild creamy cheese will do. The pesto should be fairly strong in flavour to balance this, and the tomatoes and lemon zest give it some bite.

2 slices fresh bread – multigrain
   with poppy seeds, Pugliese,
   Granary® or Cranks with
   sunflower seeds
2 tbsp ricotta or cottage cheese
1 tbsp pesto straight from the
   fridge (see *opposite*)

½ tsp freshly grated lemon zest
1 tomato
seasoning: sea salt/herb salt, freshly
   ground black pepper
small handful fresh rocket leaves

Preparing the filling:

1   Wash and wipe dry the tomato. Remember to remove the stalk and cut out any tough white core from the stalk end. Cut the tomato across its width into slices not wider than ¼ in/½ cm.

2   Wash and spin dry the rocket leaves, taking care to pick out any yellowed leaves and remove excessively stalky bits.

Assembling the sandwich:

1   Spread 2 tbsp ricotta or cottage cheese over the bottom slice of bread.
2   Spread 1 tbsp pesto over the cheese.
3   Sprinkle ½ tsp lemon zest over the pesto.
4   Cover with slices of tomato.
5   Season.
6   Cover with rocket.
7   Top with the second slice of bread, press down gently but firmly and slice in half.

★   *You can buy sundried tomato paste in most supermarkets; try it in place of the pesto.*

Pesto

Classic Italian pesto (*pesto* means pounded i.e. in a mortar and pestle) consists of fresh basil, pinenuts, olive oil, garlic, Parmesan and/or pecorino cheese. There are many good ready-made pestos available – check the colour carefully. Pesto should be a wonderful bright green colour with a fairly coarse texture: those which have faded to a khaki brown sludge are to be avoided. Sainsbury's Fresh Pesto Sauce is good, and most Italian delicatessens sell their own pesto made on the premises.

It must be stored in the fridge if you want to use it for sandwiches. Because of its high olive oil content it can get quite sloppy if warm, and is therefore difficult to use in sandwiches. However, use it straight from the fridge and it will spread nicely and by the time it warms up the ricotta cheese will have acted as a blotter. (Anyway you'll have eaten the sandwich by then!)

If you want to make pesto yourself (and as long as you have a food processor) here's how:

2 oz/55 g very fresh basil leaves, washed and gently dried with kitchen paper
1 oz /30 g pinenuts
1 fresh fat firm clove garlic, peeled, crushed and chopped
4 tbsp olive oil

1 heaped tsp butter, softened to room temperature
$\frac{1}{2}$ oz/15 g freshly grated Parmesan cheese
$\frac{1}{2}$ oz/15 g freshly grated pecorino cheese

Put the basil leaves, pinenuts, garlic and 1 tablespoon of the olive oil in the food processor. Process for half a minute then add the rest of the olive oil in a steady stream and finally the softened butter. Pour this creamy mixture into a bowl and add the grated cheeses. Mix these in by hand using a metal spoon (this gives the authentic coarse texture).

This will give you enough fresh pesto for 2 sandwiches and a brilliant pasta sauce for 2. (Spoon the pesto over freshly cooked steaming hot pasta, adding a tablespoon of the hot water in which the pasta has been cooked in order to dilute it a little.)

★ 33 **SALAMI, RICOTTA, RED ONION,** Serves 1
TOMATO, BLACK OLIVES

Try to avoid the vacuum-packed ready sliced salami, as it is invariably greasy. Instead choose something like Salami di Milano from the deli counter and ask for it to be sliced extra fine.

2 slices of fresh bread, buttered if you like
1 heaped tbsp ricotta or mascarpone cheese
4 red onion rings
2 oz/55 g salami, finely sliced

1 tbsp de-stoned black olives or tapenade (see *page 125*)
1 beef tomato
seasoning: sea salt/herb salt, freshly ground black pepper
small handful lettuce mix – Cos, radicchio

Preparing the filling:

1   Remove the skin-like rind from the slices of salami.
2   Peel the papery outside skin from the red onion. Cutting across the onion, slice off the top ¾ in/2 cm and discard. Cut 2 slices, not wider than about ⅛ in/2 mm. Take the 4 largest circles and set them aside. (Wrap the rest of the onion in clingfilm and store it in the fridge, it will keep for several days.)
3   Wash and wipe dry the tomato. Remember to remove the stalk and cut out any tough white core from the stalk end. Slice the tomato across its width into slices not wider than ¼ in/½ cm.
4   Remove the stones from the black olives (see *page 15 for notes on olives*). Chop the olives roughly.
5   Wash and spin dry the lettuce mix, taking care to remove any over-large stalks and any discoloured or limp leaves.

Assembling the sandwich:

1 Spread 1 heaped tbsp ricotta or mascarpone cheese over the bottom slice of bread.

2 Arrange 4 circles of red onion over the cheese.

3 Arrange the salami slices so that they cover the cheese.

4 Scatter 1 tbsp chopped black olives or spread 1 tbsp tapenade over the salami.

5 Cover the olives/tapenade with slices of beef tomato.

6 Season.

7 Cover with lettuce.

8 Top with the second slice of bread, press down gently but firmly and slice in half.

★ *If you want to give this sandwich an extra kick, spread a teaspoon of Dijon mustard over the ricotta cheese before you add the salami.*

34

ROAST BEEF, MUSTARD AND HORSERADISH SAUCE, ROCKET AND TOMATO

We prefer roast beef cooked rare – it is totally delicious and juicy when it's cold. If you are slicing left-over roast beef at home, use an impeccably sharp knife and slice the beef as thin as possible. If you are buying from a deli counter, ask for the beef to be sliced extra fine. You can also use carpaccio (very finely sliced raw beef) for this sandwich. If preparing carpaccio at home, make sure the beef is very cold before you try to slice it.

Serve this on Ciabatta bread, allowing a third of a loaf per person.

⅓ Ciabatta loaf, split like a pitta
   and spread with unsalted butter
2 oz/55 g finely sliced (rare) roast
   beef
1 tbsp mustard and horseradish
   sauce (see *opposite*)

1 tomato
seasoning: sea salt/herb salt, freshly
   ground black pepper
small handful fresh rocket

Preparing the filling:

1   Wash and spin dry the rocket, taking care to remove any thick stalks and any discoloured or limp leaves.

2   Wash and wipe dry the tomato. Remember to remove the stalk and cut out any tough white core from the stalk end. Cut the tomato across its width into slices no wider than ¼ in/½ cm.

Assembling the sandwich:

1   Arrange the roast beef so it covers the bottom piece of bread.

2   Spread 1 tbsp mustard and horseradish sauce over the beef.

3   Cover with slices of tomato.

4   Season.

5   Cover with rocket.

6   Cover with the top half of the ciabatta loaf.*

★ You could spread a heaped tablespoon of salsa verde (see page 85) on the top slice of bread before placing it face down on top of the sandwich. In which case you could leave out the rocket. This is especially good if you're not eating it immediately. Wrap the sandwich tightly in greaseproof paper to keep it fresh and to hold in the filling.

Mustard and Horseradish Sauce

6 tbsp mayonnaise

2 tbsp Dijon mustard

1 tbsp horseradish

2 tsp Worcester sauce

2 tsp fresh lemon juice

Mix everything together in a clean jam jar. This will give you enough for quite a few sandwiches. Stored in the fridge, with a lid, this will keep for a week.

35

ROAST BEEF, BALSAMIC VINEGAR-SOAKED ROCKET, CREAM CHEESE

Use cold rare roast beef or carpaccio as described at the top of page 130 and slice it very very fine. For the cream cheese use a mild goats' cheese, such as Innes, or ricotta or Philadelphia.

2 slices fresh bread, spread with
unsalted butter (also delicious
on freshly baked baguette,
Ciabatta or a crusty roll)
2 tbsp creamy goats' cheese
handful fresh rocket

pinch sea salt
1 tbsp balsamic vinegar
2 oz/55 g finely sliced rare roast
beef
freshly ground black pepper

Preparing the filling:

1   Wash and spin dry the rocket, taking care to remove any large stalks and any discoloured or limp leaves. Tear the leaves in half and put in a bowl with a pinch of sea salt and a tablespoon of balsamic vinegar.
2   Toss the rocket, using your hands, so that it is thoroughly coated with the balsamic vinegar. Leave it to stand for 5–10 minutes.
3   Just before making the sandwich, take the rocket from the bowl and sqeeze gently to remove any surplus vinegar. (You can use the vinegar left in the bowl for your next salad dressing.)

Assembling the sandwich:

1   Spread 2 tbsp creamy goats' cheese over the bottom slice of bread and prick the spread surface with a fork – this is to allow some of the balsamic vinegar to soak in.
2   Arrange the balsamic vinegar-soaked rocket on top of the cheese.
3   Layer the slices of roast beef on top of the rocket.
4   Season with freshly ground black pepper.
5   Top with the second slice of bread, press down gently but firmly and slice in half.

This voucher can be exchanged for the sandwich of your choice up to £2. Simply hand it in at any of our branches.

★

If you would like to speak to me or one of my colleagues regarding anything to do with **PRET A MANGER,** please feel free to call on 0171 827 6320.

Julian Metcalfe

★ PRET A MANGER ® ★ PRET A MANGER ®

THIS VOUCHER ENTITLES THE HOLDER TO A

FREE SANDWICH

★ OF YOUR CHOICE ★

Up to £2 © Photocopies not acceptable

FREE SANDWICH

PRET A MANGER ★ PRET A MANGER ★

Up to £2 © Photocopies not acceptable

173 Wardour Street W1
Selfridges, Oxford Street W1
18 Hanover Street W1
7 Marylebone High Street W1
63 Tottenham Court Road W1
Great Marleborough St. W1
163 Picadilly W1
298 Regent Street W1
54/56 Oxford Street W1
24 Berkeley Street W1
120 Baker Street W1
27 Islington High Street N1
8/10 King Street, Hammersmith W6
93a George Street, Croydon
77/78 St Martins Lane WC2
421/422 The Strand WC2
The National Gallery WC2
319 High Holborn WC1
240 High Holborn WC1
122 High Holborn WC1
44 New Oxford Street WC1
17 Eldon Street EC2
1 Finsbury Avenue EC2
140 Bishopsgate EC2
Lloyd's of London EC3
The Tower of London EC3
74 Fleet Street EC4
28 Fleet Street EC4
47 Bow Lane EC4
12 Kingsgate Parade SW1
21 Crown Passage SW1
75B Victoria Street SW3
80 Kings Road SW3
61 Beauchamp Place SW3
Station Arcade Kensington High St. W8
The Queensmere Centre, Slough
Terminal 1, Heathrow Airport
2 Cornmarket Street, Oxford